PRINCE
IMP *of the* PERVERSE

by

BARNEY HOSKYNS

Virgin

A Virgin Book
Published in 1988
by the Paperback Division of
W.H. Allen & Co Plc
44 Hill Street
London W1X 8LB

Copyright © 1988 by Barney Hoskyns

Typeset by Phoenix Photosetting, Chatham
Printed in Great Britain by Adlard & Son Ltd

Cover by The Design Clinic
Design by Neil Watkinson

Cover photographs: Rex Features

ISBN 0 86369 254 0

ACKNOWLEDGMENTS

Thanks to Barbara Charone at WEA in London, Melanie
Ciccone at Warner Brothers in New York, *Smash Hits*,
Will Self, Keith Patchel, Charles Melcher, Annene Kaye,
Laura Levine, Tim Carr, Nick Kent, Max Kirsten,
Fred Dellar, Robin Jackson.

And to Cat, Alison and Neil for putting up with me.

PRINCE

IMP *of the* PERVERSE

by

BARNEY HOSKYNS

Contents

Introduction

"He's got something he wants to communicate.
I don't know
if it's something you could write down."

(William Blinn, co-writer of *Purple Rain*)

By common consent, Prince Rogers Nelson is one of the few really significant figures in pop music today. He elevates it to a level of intensity and ingenuity that makes the competition look tired and contrived. Nine albums on from his debut in 1978, he has consolidated his position as a leader and innovator who shows no sign of flagging.

There are no particular camps of people who admire him. Almost everyone who follows popular music at all is intrigued by him, excited to know what he'll do next. He is self-assured enough to try anything, continually wandering off on tangents that simply don't occur to others. Industry-generated pop fluff is as dead and homogenised to him as it is to most of us. "What's missing from pop music is danger", he observed in November 1982. "There's no excitement and mystery – people sneaking out and going to these forbidden concerts by Elvis Presley or Jimi Hendrix . . ."

The first time I saw Prince live, in New York in 1981, it stirred up this sense of the forbidden in a way which directly recalled a foundational pop moment for me: the night I saw Marc Bolan singing 'Get It On' on *Top Of The Pops* in 1971. There was the same hypnotic sexual charge, the same sinister campness, the same musical spell. The experience was so electrifying that I, like many others, could talk of little else for weeks after. Since then his music has become even more compelling, more "rich and strange", than any of us dared hope. When a Prince record comes on the radio today it's as if something pure and eccentrically real has pierced through the stultifying blanket of over-produced machine music. Where synthesizers dehumanise most musicians today, Prince humanises synthesizers. Where most producers build pedestrian songs into mountains of reverb and overdub, Prince strips masterpieces down to irreducible bases of funk and melody – who else could have made 'When Doves Cry', 'Kiss', 'Sign 'O' The Times'?

Prince is the last great *individual* surfing the mainstream of pop, the last of a brilliant and erratic breed that includes the various progenitors of his persona: Little Richard, Stevie Wonder, Sly Stone, Jimi Hendrix, George Clinton. These are people who've used and abused the pop circus, jesters who've danced round it and made it mean something when it suited them. They are innovators who chose to play it UNSAFE and reaped the greater rewards for doing so. People like them have more fun than people like Madonna and Michael Jackson.

If pop ever had a mandate, in the eighties it has forfeited it. To provoke, to amuse, to disturb, to celebrate: these were some of its aims (and achievements) in the fifties and sixties and seventies. All pop is about today is stardom itself: being popular. And so suffused is it by its own history that all the boys and girls clambering feverishly aboard the merry-go-round only desire to be composites of former idols. If you've got it, flaunt it, but if you haven't got it, flaunt that instead. As they said of punk rock, anyone can do it. Even Madonna.

What does our glitzy, vapid pop culture say about the world in the late eighties? It says that an awful lot of people want their 15-Warhol-minutes' worth. It says that a lot of 19-year-old boys think they need the adulation of 14-year-old girls in order to be happy. And it says that, all things considered, "entertainment" has become a pretty sanitised business.

Pop has been drained of its perversity, its madness. (And no one writes good tunes any more.) We must hold fast to the likes of Prince, a petite and extraordinary genius from the amorphous Midwest of America, and trust that others will follow.

Chapter One

"Loneliness, Poverty And Sex"

Prince's childhood was the archetypal one of the star: LONELY INADEQUATE BOY REINVENTS HIMSELF IN THE PRIVACY OF HIS OWN MIND. The myth of pop starts here, in front of the bedroom mirror. The runt of the litter makes good; the silent nonentity grows up to be a sex god while the class bully ends up as the neighbourhood postman. It's some kind of rock 'n' roll justice.

Prince Rogers Nelson – "Princess" to his less charitable classmates – grew up with this vision in his heart, this certainty that he would rise above his persecutors. Teased for being so short, he would become a giant. He knew it, too, from the day in 1963 when (aged five) he watched his jazz pianist father play a dancehall matinée show in Austin, Minnesota. Later he recalled: "My mother drove by to tell him something and I was supposed to wait in the car, but I snuck into the hall to watch. I couldn't believe it, people were screaming. I remember thinking 'these people think my dad is great' and I wanted to be part of that. Then a dancer spotted me, grabbed me, shook me up and took me back to the car. Her

name was Kit. She was pretty." This is Prince's primal scene: the atmosphere is intoxicating, his own father is provoking screams, and the dancer is pretty. (Perhaps all the Vanities and Apollonias descend from Kit. One can only imagine the erotic glee with which *le petit prince* kicked and struggled in her arms.) Returning to John Hay Elementary School in Minneapolis, the boy has the illicit spectacle firmly stored in his memory.

Prince's memories of his childhood are very precious to him, not because they are happy (they're not), but because they are so integral a part of his myth. As *Melody Maker*'s Steve Sutherland wrote afer interviewing him in June 1981, "things like his father leaving home, his brother flitting in and out of the slam and a period lodging with his sister all seem to hold a fathomless fascination for him, and he constantly calls upon his past, almost endowing it with some spiritual significance as he struggles to explain the motives behind his music." For someone purportedly so reclusive and secret, Prince has actually said a great deal about his childhood – quite apart from blowing it up on the big screen in *Purple Rain*. On the surface it probably wasn't so different from the average childhood in the black neighbourhood of North Minneapolis. John Nelson was a musician but his income came primarily from working as a plaster moulder at the giant Honeywell electronics plant. Like many young blacks in the fifties, he'd settled in the predominantly white city of Minneapolis because there was lots of work available. Prince's mother, Mattie Shaw, came from Baton Rouge, Louisiana, marrying Nelson after singing part-time with his Prince Rogers Trio. Temperamentally they were very different: "My mom's the wild side of me", says Prince. "My dad's real serene."

The boy was born on 7 June 1958 in Minneapolis' Mount Sinai Hospital. 'Prince' was his father's stage name and his father's choice; Mattie, in protest, later called him "Skipper". (Is it any wonder a boy has problems when both his parents give him names barely fit for a dog?) Whether his early years were as traumatic as the scenes of domestic violence in *Purple Rain* might suggest is unclear. Certainly the incompatibility between his quiet, music-obsessed father and his light-hearted mother was a real one, and John Nelson left Mattie and their children Prince and Tyka (born 1960) when the boy was only seven. "He played me some of his father's music", recalls William Blinn, writer of *Purple Rain*, "and when he talked about his father's life you could tell that was the key to what he's about. It was as if he were sorting out his own mystery."

"Musicians, depending on how serious they are, they're really moody", says Prince. "Sometimes they need a lot of space. They want everything just right. My father was a great deal like that. And Ma wanted a husband *per se*." Indeed, Mattie even resented the musical hold Nelson

"Why do you have to know who I am?"

Prince in 1977

had over their son; calling the boy "Skipper" was her way of denying that hold. Yet as Prince was later to sing in 'When Doves Cry', "Maybe I'm just like my father, too bold/Maybe you're just like my mother, she's never satisfied . . ." He may not have idolised his father, but he inherited many of his character traits. As Nelson Sr said in 1984, "I spend a lot of time by myself, writing and composing music. That's the most important thing to me. I don't care to meet strangers." It might have been Prince talking, and the son later paid tribute to the father when he used 'Father's Song' in *Purple Rain* and two John Nelson tunes on the *Parade* album.

Nelson was inadvertently responsible for his son's first faltering musical steps by simple virtue of the fact that when he moved out he left a grand piano in the house. The boy's first dabbling was on this instrument, picking out the theme tunes from TV shows like *Batman*, *Dragnet* and *The Man From U.N.C.L.E.* (*Purple Rain*'s 'Darling Nikki' would later combine the themes of *The Munsters* and *The Addams Family*.) "I had a pretty good idea of what the piano was all about by the time I was eight", Prince says, though he never bothered with lessons. Of his one subsequent music tutorial (on the guitar), he says: "I did what I wanted and that kind of pissed off the teacher. I don't even like the idea of training. I don't feel anybody can teach you an art. I don't think the basics can be taught either. Maybe that's naïve and mental, but that's my way." The *wunderkind*'s first performances were at talent shows in the 4th and 5th grades at John Hay Elementary. At nine years old he was playing original piano pieces in front of an audience. "I never *sang* in talent shows", he remembers. "I never thought I *could* sing. My speaking voice was so deep it hurt to sing. I had

to sing in a high voice, but Lord knows I didn't want to be laughed at, so I would only sing in my *boudoir!*" Even in the Seventh Day Adventist Church he attended every week, he was "afraid" to sing. "Deep down I wanted to but I guess I was a little shy."

Aside from brief moments of musical glory, Prince's school years were pretty miserable ones. Chronically introverted, he was continually the butt of jokes and nicknames – the cruellest of the latter was "Butcher Dog", used because his peers decreed that he looked like a German Shepherd. "I hated being around people", he says. "I didn't like the fact that they seemed to know more about the world than me. I was considered strange. I recall having a lot of strange dreams. I spent a lot of time alone and I turned to music. In some ways it was more important than people." Like many a natural introvert, however, Prince would occasionally explode into manic exhibitionism, imitating personality wrestlers like The Crusher and Mad Dog Vachon in the schoolyard. A classmate called Paul Mitchell recalls how Prince would "get on people's nerves seeking attention."

Life at home didn't improve matters. Not only was the family considerably worse off with John Nelson's departure, but Mattie remarried and Prince took an instant dislike to his stepfather, Hayward Baker. "He dealt with a lot of materialistic things. He would bring us presents all the time rather than sit down and talk with us or give us companionship. I would say all the things I disliked about him rather than tell him what I really needed. Which was a mistake, and kind of hurt our relationship." One present for which Prince was forever grateful, however, was being taken by Baker to see a James Brown show in Minneapolis at the age of ten. The memory of this is at least as indelible as that of watching his father perform five years before. "My stepdad lifted me on to the stage", he said in a short MTV interview in 1985, "and I danced a little bit until the bodyguard took me off." Miles Davis, who collaborated with him on an unreleased version of 'If I Was Your Girlfriend', says Prince was obsessed by the show for weeks afterwards, working first on Brown's spellbinding dance routines, then on the drum patterns (using an old box of newspapers), and finally on the trademark guitar riffs. But the experience was formative not just musically: "The reason I liked James Brown so much is that on my way backstage I saw some of the finest girls I'd ever seen in my life." Brown, then at the height of his Black Power charisma, immediately symbolised for Prince a more personal kind of power. Not only would Prince have beautiful women backstage, he would also drill his musicians with Brown's ruthless discipline and fine them when they were high or late for rehearsals. The tour manager of the 1980/81 *Dirty Mind* tour said Prince was like a "little general".

Another formative event at this time for Prince was discovering a hidden cache of pornographic novels under his mother's bed. Mattie has denied the story but Prince claims this is where it all started and recalls trying to write some of his own smut. Inevitably the books became part of the fantasy world he dwelt in, stored away until they could explode in his music. Like everything else the experience was bottled up inside. Prince entered the uncertain and confusing world of adolescence looking like a sullen version of Michael Jackson – like many young blacks of the time he sported an enormous Jackson 5 Afro hairstyle. At 12 he ran away

from home for the first time, thus beginning a long and rootless period. "I was constantly running from family to family. It was nice on the one hand, because I always had a new family, but I didn't like being shuffled around." After staying on the south side of Minneapolis with his father (who bought him an electric guitar that was "bigger than I was"), he moved in with an aunt called Olivia, but she and the guitar didn't get on and Prince found himself homeless once more.

The family who eventually took him in and gave him a proper home were the Andersons, friends of his parents. Prince knew their youngest son André from church but didn't know that the boy's father had once played bass in the Prince Rogers Trio. Bernadette Anderson, a cheerful and good-hearted woman who already had plenty of her own children to look after, welcomed Prince into her North Minneapolis home and put him in a room with André, later to rename himself André Cymone as the bass player in Prince's touring band. André remembers Prince as being meticulously tidy when he first arrived: where he himself was already a small-time delinquent, Prince "didn't even cuss" and kept his side of the bedroom immaculately neat. "He kept himself to himself", remembers Bernadette Anderson. "He never said much, but he was an emotional volcano that could erupt at any moment. The fury showed itself when schoolfriends teased him about his height, because he loved basketball and you need to be tall for that. They were very cruel." It was particularly galling to Prince that his stepbrother Duane was so much taller and better at sports than he was. Nonetheless, at 5' 1", he played in the junior varsity basketball team at Central High School. As a pupil, too, he

*The new Stevie Wonder
proves he can do it all*

was bright enough. "I always had a pretty high academic level, I guess", he told *New York Rocker*, though elsewhere he's said he "never gave extra, which in their eyes was being a rebellious brat."

While it's probably too simplistic to say that André Anderson corrupted the 13-year-old Prince, it would certainly appear that he introduced him to a new group of friends and most particularly to sex. "Between the ages of 14 and 17 we shared maybe 20 girls", says André. "It didn't matter who went first. We didn't like to be bored, and it was a challenge to get these girls to participate in some lewd activity." It's more than possible that these salacious titbits were concocted by the Prince camp simply to bolster the whole X-rated *Dirty Mind* image of the period. Prince himself told John Morthland that after an initial sexual experience at 13 his relationships were all platonic till he turned 17. But certainly sex was becoming as big an obsession for Prince as his music: "I saw an analyst once because I was wondering why I was so sexual-minded and why I wanted to go against the grain so much, because it got me into a lotta trouble a lotta times."

Prince recalls that the clique of kids that gathered around André and himself "got together mainly for music and sex. Some of us were into drugs, though not a lot. Music was only about a fifth of it. I liked to paint, for example. I wouldn't really call it a gang. We stole things but we didn't have fights. It was interesting. You learn a lot. It's like . . . psychiatry or something. People constantly telling you how they feel about you and things like that." Surviving on a diet of Quaker Oats — "it saved a lot of us from malnutrition", he says — Prince began jamming on songs he'd written

19

with André. André's mother had given him the basement of the house as his personal lair, and the new freedom and privacy produced a spurt of creative energy. He installed a Magnus chord organ and decorated the room with mirrors and rabbit furs. One evening he had a girl with him and Bernadette allowed her to stay the night. "After that I knew it was OK to explore whatever I wanted down there. Things weren't forbidden anymore. I wrote a ton of songs – my brain was free of everything. I didn't have anything to worry about, and that's when I realised that music could express what you were feeling. It came out in my songs – loneliness, poverty and sex." The basement became a kind of laboratory of desires and ideas.

It need hardly be said that before Prince put it on the map Minneapolis was not the hippest music city in America. Growing up in this chilly Midwestern town several hours northwest of Chicago had serious drawbacks, not the least of which was the virtual absence of black-oriented radio stations. (In a city where only 5 per cent of the population was black, that is hardly surprising – as Prince himself says, "I grew up on the borderline, I never grew up in one particular culture".) But growing up free of established musical traditions has advantages: as Prince observed in January 1980, "Minneapolis is so far behind other major cities in the country it forces you to create your own sound. There's no point in copying other trends because by the time they get here they're out of date." If the city had pop roots at all they were almost exclusively white. The sixties coughed up two legendary Midwest garage bands, The Trashmen (with 'Surfin' Bird') and The Castaways (with 'Liar Liar') and many lesser ones – The High Spirits, for instance, who included Prince's future man-

Little Richard and James Brown:

"I see more of Little Richard than myself in Prince",

said James.

"I guess he wants to be like me – but you see, I don't do anything vulgar onstage."

ager Owen Husney and hit with a grungy version of 'Turn On Your Lovelight' on Soma Records.

Bob Dylan (né Zimmerman) came from Hebbing, Minnesota, passed through Minneapolis, and headed quickly for New York. A folk and blues scene thrived for some years on the campus of the University of Minnesota, the most famous exponents of which were the trio Koerner, Ray & Glover. (Tony Glover subsequently went on in 1967 to become the DJ on KDWB's *Midnight Show*, counteracting the Top 40 WDGY station by playing the likes of Hendrix and The Doors.) Prince claims he never had a radio or a record player and so missed out on the psychedelic sixties. Perhaps that's why he later became so enamoured and entranced by them in the eighties. "I never got a chance to check out Hendrix and the rest of them because they were dead by the time I was getting really serious." In the early seventies the city was loosely divided between acoustic guitar virtuosi like Leo Kottke and Michael Johnson and primordial heavy metal bands like Crow and Cottage Cheese. Aside from one or two bars downtown, the live scene was centred in ballrooms like the Purple Barn and the Purple Cigar (Prince's fondness for the colour is not unprecedented in Minneapolis – even the Minnesota Vikings' colour is purple), where bands would churn out Top 40 covers all night. There wasn't a lot to inspire a 14-year-old black *wunderkind*.

Prince persevered in the basement. Having mastered the piano and the guitar, he got to grips with bass guitar and saxophone. "I learned how to play many things out of boredom", he says. "Once you learn piano, everything else falls into place." In 1972, a cousin of Prince's called Charles Smith asked him to play guitar in his band and asked André Anderson to play bass. Smith, the drummer and lead singer, later said that the two friends had a twin-like sixth sense playing together. Bringing in other members of the "clique" to complete the line-up – André's sister Linda on keyboards, Terry Jackson and William Daugherty on percussion – they called the band Grand Central. The name seems to have been a loose one; in an interview in the Central High *Pioneer* of 13 February 1976, the band is referred to as Grand Central Corporation, while four years later, in a *Musician* piece by Steve Perry, it's called Grand Central Junction. Possibly these variations were hybrids of bands Prince and his cronies came to admire: the power rock trio Grand Funk Railroad, for example, and Graham Central Station, a funk offshoot from Prince's beloved Sly And The Family Stone. Sly And The Family Stone songs – 'Everybody Is A Star' was a particular favourite, and an undoubted influence on *Purple Rain*'s 'Baby I'm A Star' – featured prominently in the Top 40-oriented sets Grand Central used to play. "There was quite a lot of Sly Stone stuff we used to do", says Prince. "I really liked it when he'd have a hit, because it would give us an excuse to play them." (Sly dropped into the Record Plant in Sausalito, California when Prince was recording his first album; the young neophyte clammed up in terror.)

Dressed in self-made suede suits, with each member's astrological sign sewn on the back (*very* 1972!), Grand Central began gigging on Saturday afternoons on the lawns of neighbours in the area. The band became, in Prince's words, "a roving jukebox", playing the hits of the day at YMCAs, talent shows, and high school "sock hops". "It got pretty sickening", he says, "because I had to dissect these songs and teach each part to each person. So when the artist got a hit again I knew exactly what was gonna go down in the music and it was just a turn-off." Although Charles Smith occasionally sang, Prince says that until he went to Central High in 1973 the group mainly performed instrumental versions of Top 40 hits. Curiously, he told Robert Hilburn of the *LA Times* that he never wanted to be a frontman, and that "it felt kinda spooky to be at the mike alone."

At school Prince's self-esteem improved with his new-found glory as a guitar hero. He admits that performing was a way to compete with his taller, more athletic peers. A high point was playing the homecoming dance at Central High, where fellow students included Brown Mark (then Mark Brown), Terry Lewis (later of The Time and Jam & Lewis Productions) and Terry Casey of Paisley Park band Mazarati. Classmate Ronnie Robbins recalls that Prince was an outstanding music student: "He'd walk into a jazz ensemble class even though he wasn't enrolled in it, pick up an instrument, kill it, and just walk out." He also enrolled in several classes to learn the business side of the music industry, telling Bernadette Anderson that "come what may" he would have a job that involved music. Other people remember a strange and silent teenager sitting in the school hallways playing Maria Muldaur's 'Midnight At The Oasis' on a jumbo acoustic guitar. (Muldaur was just one of several folkie jazz ladies Prince admired, Joni Mitchell being the most important.) As early as 1974 he was attracting attention as a "promising talent" – in an interview with the *Minnesota Daily* he said that he wanted to perform choreographed dance routines onstage, "but only ones without spins – they make me nauseated." Interestingly, he also

stated that he would one day record jazz under a different name.

Shortly after Prince went to Central High School, the band changed their name to Champagne. Not only did the line-up then expand, but Charles Smith left and was replaced on drums by a cousin of William Daugherty's called Morris Day. Overcoming his fears of being in the spotlight, Prince took over the role of leader and began slipping his own songs into the cover-dominated repertoire. "I really liked to hear the band play a song I'd written", he remembers. "There were a lot of love songs and some real crazy ones, campy stuff. I wrote a song about spitting, which was real dumb and crude, but I was young then. We used to laugh a lot. I liked writing fantasies, fairytales. I used to make up things a lot, different situations I'd put myself into, and pretend I was that particular person . . . I dealt in fantasy a lot because I spent a lot of time alone. That's what my first two albums were about.

"It was sickening to have an audience walk out when you went into an original, then come back in when you got to Top Ten stuff. André was writing the real popular stuff. I was real torn. A lot of the songs I never showed to the band. I only showed them the ones that had a beat, never the ones about insane painters in asylums or about death." (!) Of the songs Prince did show to the band, the majority were already employing the sexual shock tactics which came to the fore in later years. One of them, 'Machine', was so crudely explicit about the female sex organs it had teenage audiences "covering their faces in embarrassment".

Prince has claimed that he had no musical idols at this time, but Minneapolis writer Jon Bream says the members of Champagne would

Some of the ingredients in Prince's strange brew: Smokey Robinson, Sly Stone, Carlos Santana, Stevie Wonder, Jimi Hendrix

listen to KQRS, the progressive Minneapolis station that played everything from the Allman Brothers to Edgar Winter. If Prince styled himself on anyone, it was guitar heroes like Carlos Santana rather than soul superstars like Stevie Wonder – he even signed 'Carlos Santana' in a friend's high-school yearbook. Of influences that might seem more pertinent to his eventual fusion of funk and rock, he says, "I've never really sat down and listened to Sly Stone, unless a friend had it on at a party. I've never studied him or Funkadelic, though I met George Clinton recently and it does seem we have some things in common." (Clinton recently signed a deal with Prince's Paisley Park label.) The boy's biggest fear was of being influenced by music that was already out of date. He was convinced that every new trend arrived in Minneapolis six months after it had been everywhere else, and that if he imitated what he heard

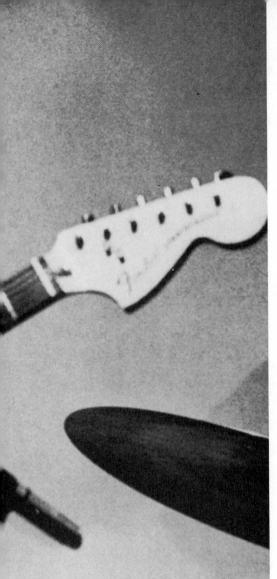

*A black teen pin-up in
the making: Prince
recording demos in 1977*

and Philadelphia Story formed and a bar called The Flame opened downtown. As he told Detroit DJ The Electrifying Mojo in November 1986, "radio was dead, the discos was dead, even the ladies was kind of dead, and I knew if we wanted to make some noise I was going to have to get something together. Which is what we did – we put together a few bands and turned it into Uptown." Despite being underage, Champagne managed to get gigs at The Flame and competed against other black bands like Cohesion. The strongest competition came from a funk outfit called Flyte Tyme, co-founded in 1974 by bassist Terry Lewis and drummer Jellybean Johnson and featuring a young Alexander O'Neal on vocals. The two co-founders had played together in a band called Wars Of Armageddon and formed Flyte Tyme initially around the voice of Cynthia Johnson (later the singer on Lipps Inc's 1980 hit 'Funkytown'.) The rivalry between them and Champagne was amusingly played out in *Purple Rain* ten years later. Champagne, meanwhile, were briefly managed by Morris Day's mother LaVonne Daugherty, who'd had some experience in the business but lacked the resources to get them a deal. As they progressed, they moved further into dance styles, dubbing their sound "futuristic funk" and covering songs by the likes of Larry Graham, Grover Washington, and Midwest funkers The Ohio Players. Uptown was finally on the map.

Madonna Ciccone has said of Prince: "I can relate to him. He has a chip on his shoulder. He's competitive, from the Midwest, a screwed-up home, and he has something to prove." In 1976, he was getting ready to prove it.

25

on the radio he would end up sounding "prehistoric". "I dreaded that more than anything, because there was a lot of competition in Minneapolis. All the bands jammed together and if you were to play another person's lick from a record you got ridiculed so bad that you never did it again."

The scene in Minneapolis by the mid-seventies was what Prince fondly came to call "Uptown". Black bands like Sweet Taste Of Sin

Chapter Two

A Boy King

Jimmy Jam, ex-member of The Time and one half of the brilliant Jam & Lewis production team, remembers the "Uptown" scene thus: "Black musicians weren't allowed to play in the nice clubs. So what happened was that there was no way to get comfortable up here, playing the clubs and getting their two or three hundred dollars a week. The black musicians didn't have a chance, so they aspired to doing something out of the realm of playing clubs. That was to do demo tapes and try and move on to a national level. That was the motivating factor."

Prince certainly knew in 1976 that it was time to go beyond Minneapolis. As recent protegée Jill Jones puts it, "you sit there in the Midwest and think 'How'm I gonna get discovered here?'" Ex-Revolution guitarist Dez Dickerson once said that Minneapolis is "comparatively unsegregated", but bar owners still feared racial trouble if they booked black bands and Champagne had to make do playing small black clubs like Nacirema. The boy's first taste of the music business beyond gigging in clubs came when a

Brooklyn artist called Pepe Willie came to town to record a session for Polydor with the veteran Motown producer Hank Cosby. Pepe had married a cousin of Prince's and needed a guitarist for the session at Sound 80, then Minneapolis' only quality 24-track studio. (Leo Kottke used it and Bob Dylan recorded the great *Blood On The Tracks* album there.) Singing on the session was one Colonel Abrams, later to hit with songs like 'Trapped'. He recalls that Prince was "just a little guy in jeans, a plain shirt and an Afro. He was always serious, very quiet – and very suspicious. You never knew what he was thinking." Abrams co-wrote a song with Prince, 'Love Love Love', but says that the 18-year-old "just could not sing – I had to do it all." More galling for Prince was the fact that Hank Cosby dismissed his ideas out of hand and wasn't interested when he wanted to redo his part.

Some of the out-takes from the session were later issued by Pepe Willie on the Hot Pink label (*The Minneapolis Genius: 94 East*) and featured Prince's guitar work in what Stuart Cosgrove described as "an oddball meeting of

jazz, free rock, and synthesized dance music." The six tracks are almost all instrumental, whether because Willie took Colonel Abrams' vocals off the mix is not altogether clear. The tacky cover is predictably purple, with the obligatory dove perched in the centre. Prince has said that Champagne first demo'd at a Minneapolis studio called ASI, but there is no record of this tape. What *is* known is that shortly after the Pepe Willie session Prince approached Chris Moon, an English-born engineer who promoted local gigs for KQRS and owned a small 16-track studio in Minneapolis called Moon Sound. When Moon discovered how multi-talented Prince was, he offered him the chance to learn and master the studio in return for help on songs and jingles. "We had an arrangement that we would split 50/50 whatever material might become successful", says Moon. "At the time it was a long-range thing. So we worked together about eight months writing songs. I taught him the studio."

Moon recalls that he'd give Prince the studio keys and let him have the run of the place on weekends. "That's where he got his experience in multi-tracking, putting all the instruments down himself." It was a crucial break for Prince, a chance to create his own sound world free of others – he has preferred ever since to work on his own. "Interaction happens more so when I'm alone than when I work with someone else. When I do bass tracks I always know what the drummer is gonna do – I'm right inside his head. It sounds a lot different when I record with other people." Perhaps it was these first signs of Prince's solipsistic predilection for playing with himself that alienated the rest of his band and led to its collapse. It seems clear that he began thinking of himself as a solo act at this

time. (Moon remembers him deeply absorbed in practising his autograph – with the trademark heart over the 'i' – at the studio.)

Prince recorded five main songs at Moon Sound: 'Soft And Wet', co-written with Moon and eventually Prince's first Warner Brothers single, 'My Love Is Forever' (also on the first album), 'Aces', 'Make It Through The Storm', and the infamous 'Machine'. 'Soft And Wet' was crucial, a blueprint for the lightly clipped funk style of future hits like 'I Wanna Be Your Lover' and 'Sexy Dancer'. It also defined Prince's early eroticism: Chris Moon had had some experience in advertising and came up with the concept of "implied naughty sexuality" to capture the boy's attitude. Actually it hit the nail on the head – Andy Schwartz of *New York Rocker* later described Prince's early style as "puppy sex", and the erotic ambience of 'Soft and Wet' is very precisely "naughty", implicit rather than

BLUES AND SOUL

explicit.

Prince was finding his musical identity in these songs – at this stage a *pot-pourri* of Sly Stone, the Jacksons, Earth Wind & Fire, and the disco sound of Sylvester. The taut syncopation came from EW&F and the Jacksons, the muted wah-wah guitar and clavinet from Sly's laid-back funk of the early seventies. As for the falsetto flutter of the voice, Prince had finally found his range: a camp but cocksure croon distilled from Sylvester, Michael Jackson, and EW&F's Philip Bailey. So Moon was a decisive influence on Prince. Not only did he realise that the boy's essential hook was sexual – "sex sells", he told him – but he quickly saw the crossover potential in Prince's straddling of styles and tastes. It was Moon, too, who advised him to drop the "Nelson" and become plain old "Prince". But there was also something of a power struggle between them: while recording

'Aces', Prince refused to redo a track that Moon didn't like, and it started a series of ego games, subtle tests of each other's power. Just as he had dispensed with a guitar teacher after one lesson at the age of eleven, so now the little primadonna was becoming too stubborn to teach.

The principal problem with the finished demo tape was that the songs were all too long, as Prince discovered when he took it to New York in the summer of 1976 to hunt for a record deal. "I was writing things that a cat with ten albums would have out", he says, "seven-minute laments that were, y'know, *gone*. I wrote like I was rich, like I had been everywhere and seen everything and been with every woman in the world." Staying with an older half-sister called Sharon – perhaps the protagonist of the notorious 'Sister' – he began touting the tape around. One of the few companies he got in to see was Atlantic, who advised him to stay in New York and "get the pulse of the music". He later recalled the effect of the city's "sinisterness", an influence perhaps on the twilight perversions of *Dirty Mind*. Sharon herself became interested in managing her half-brother, and took him to see a French producer called Danielle Mauroy. Mauroy, from Paris, was busy auditioning another act when they arrived, but they got her attention for long enough for Prince to sing an *a capella* version of 'Baby', a song about "a cat getting a girl pregnant . . ." Mauroy was impressed, and in due course made plans to record Prince using some top New York sessionmen. Prince took fright. "Danielle Mauroy had a lot of strange ideas, using tubas and cellos and such. I knew I'd have to do it myself if it was going to come out right." The Frenchwoman also made Prince a derisory publishing offer for his songs. *continued over*

31

Back in Minneapolis, meanwhile, Chris Moon was also taking the tape around. Owen Husney, a white ex-musician and tour publicist who ran an advertising agency, heard it: "Chris brought me the tape, and I thought it was very good. A little crude, the songs ran on, there was no real form to the numbers. But he was a raw talent, a rough diamond who needed to be polished up and needed the right people around him to make it." Moon and Husney contacted Prince in New York and suggested he return to Minneapolis. In September 1976, Husney formed a management company, American Artists Inc., with Minneapolis corporate attorney Gary Levinson. They immediately signed Prince and rented an office in Loring Park. "With my background in business structure and planning and Owen's creativity in public relations, advertising and merchandising, we started a programme", says Levinson, who worked for the downtown firm Robins, Davis & Lyons. "We started out with our own money in the project, but when it started to run into substantial amounts we felt it was prudent to get investors to help spread the risk a little. They were basically friends, and their legal status was as 'limited partners', whereas Owen and I had unlimited liability for everything."

The first task Husney and Levinson set themselves was to make Prince a more commercial prospect. "We talked with him about the structure of his tunes", says Husney. "They had to follow more what you hear on the radio, be put more in a commercial role. But there is some music right on the line, and you gotta cross over that line to be real. Prince, in my estimation, had crossed over." Prince himself gives Husney a lot of credit for convincing him that he couldn't continue writing "seven-minute terror

BLUES AND SOUL

"Just don't compare me to Michael Jackson . . ."

(Prince in 1981)

32

songs." "I wrote a lot of strange things back then", he said in 1979. (More songs about death and mad painters?) "I'll probably start again when I'm accepted for what I am rather than for how much money I make." He also says it was Husney who convinced him he should produce himself. "I don't know if I really agreed with him at the time, but I believed in his gusto, in *his* belief. I didn't know if I was old enough – 'producer' sounded like a big term. I didn't know. It didn't really mean that much at all." Husney put Prince on a basic $50 a week, bought him his first synthesizer, and found him an apartment with a waterbed. The two of them would go to local gigs together, Prince "looking at the players and wondering what they were thinking about", lost in a fantasy of stardom. Before the end of 1977, Husney booked Prince into Sound 80 to record new, 24-track versions of 'Soft And Wet' and 'Make It Through The Storm', plus a first recording of 'Baby'. Engineering the session was David Rivkin, like Husney an ex-member of sixties garage band The High Spirits.

Husney claims that it was he and Chris Moon who turned Prince on to synthesizers as the sound of the future. He adds that before the boy got his Oberheim 4-voice synth he was planning to record 'Baby' with horns and strings. When local keyboard wizard Roger Dumas was brought in to help Prince programme it he was making a crucial contribution to the future of the keyboard-dominated Minneapolis sound. "I got hip to polymoogs when I was working at Sound 80", Prince later recalled. "I liked them a lot then. I was trying to get away from using the conventional sound of pianos and clavinets as keyboards." The presentation of Prince had begun. As Husney says, "it took two years of a

lot of effort by a lot of people in this town to make Prince what he was, and we left no stone unturned. A record label is looking for more than just talent – we had to convince them Prince was a genius." He and Levinson approached the project with a philosophy of "pessimistic optimism", hoping for the best but not expecting it. Committing themselves to the tune of $50,000, they followed up the Sound 80 demos by putting together a limited number of exceptional quality promo packages. "We wanted something that would show Prince's multi-dimensional talent, that people would read while we were there", says Gary Levinson. "That meant you couldn't give them pages of bio and newspaper clippings. We designed a package, a calling card which took thirty seconds to read and instantly you knew there was something special there. It was very simple and a little bit dramatic, all black, heavy, nice paper, with a nice pic of Prince on the cover in black and outlined by a thin red line." In addition, the tapes were mounted on balanced brush aluminium reels.

In March 1977, the pair were ready to make their move. For the next three months they virtually commuted between Minneapolis and Los Angeles, fixing up meetings with all the major companies on the West Coast. With Husney dressed in jeans and cowboy boots and Levinson looking like the corporate lawyer he was, they made a curious pair. Hiring LA music attorney Lee Phillips, they touted Prince as an 18-year-old prodigy, a new Stevie Wonder. Husney was already building an air of secrecy around Prince to add to the hype – "I actually began that shroud of mystery . . . Prince carried it to the limits" – and his real trump card was probably the audacity of demanding that the

boy produce himself. Of the child prodigy hype, Prince later remarked (more than a little disingenuously): "That's all fabricated evidence that the management did to make it happen. I just did it as a sort of hobby, then it turned into a job, and now I do it as art." While he sat at home indulging his hobby, then, Husney and Levinson watched with bemusement as an intense bidding war developed in LA. Though RSO and ABC-Dunhill turned Prince down cold, CBS, Warner Brothers and A&M all frantically competed to sign him, the latter's Herb Alpert personally calling Husney in Minneapolis. The one reservation they all had, of course, concerned Prince producing his own first album. This was unheard of; was he really capable of it? Husney assured Russ Thyret, an old contact of his who'd become a vice-president at Warners, that he was, and Prince says they plumped for that label primarily because Thyret fought so hard for the demand to be met.

Warner Brothers decided to give the Midwest *wunderkind* a chance to prove himself in the studio. "We took him in one day, much to his chagrin", recalls Lenny Waronker, then the company's head of A&R. "We said 'Play the drums' and he played the drums and put a bass part down, a guitar part. And we just said 'Yeah fine, that's good enough'." (Also present were top Warners producers Russ Titelman and Ted Templeman, together with the old Steely Dan producer Gary Katz. All were highly impressed.) When Warners eventually came through with the winning offer, it turned out to be the biggest new artist signing of 1977 – indeed, the biggest contract for a new single artist in history beside the one Johnny Winter signed with CBS in 1969. "It was called a rags-to-riches story", laughs Husney, who upped

34

sticks with Prince and relocated for five months to the balmier climate of Mill Valley, north of San Francisco. Here, in Sausalito, was the famous Record Plant, a studio both Sly Stone and Carlos Santana had used. "We got Prince a house in San Francisco and another in LA", says Husney. "My wife [Britt] gave up her job and did laundry and cooking for him. We took care of him down to his hair." His wildest dream become reality at last, Prince spent the entire five months ensconced in the Record Plant; spent, too, nearly twice his advance on three albums. Warners had wanted Maurice White of Earth, Wind & Fire to produce, but after Husney's demands had been met agreed to limit outside interference to the presence of an "executive producer" called Tommy Vicari.

Prince resented Vicari's presence and the relationship between them was a strained one from the outset. Often working 12 hours a day, the pair were so burned out towards the end that Vicari moved out of the house they were all sharing. "He was really just an engineer", Prince told *NME*'s Chris Salewicz in June 1981. "And that caused a lot of problems, because he was versed in short cuts that I didn't want to take. That was why it took five months to make. The recording's become a little easier these days. I used to be a perfectionist – too much of one. Those ragged edges tend to be a little truer."

The album, *For You*, finally saw the light of day on 7 April 1978, and featured eight numbers plus an extraordinary intro title-piece serving as a kind of fanfare to Prince's entire career – simply the boy wonder's seraphic falsetto multi-tracked 45 times in a shimmering choral cascade that Brian Wilson of the Beach Boys would have been proud of. The LP's cover is an 'undistinguished blur, the boy's alarmed,

gazelle-like eyes staring from the midst of an enormous, gauzy Afro. The dust cover, designed by Prince, is more telling, showing him floating naked and messiah-like through space on a bizarre couch. Clutching an outsize acoustic guitar, he is flanked by two ghostly, transparent profiles of himself – a quasi-religious image of the trinity. Look carefully, too, and you'll see a telltale dove fluttering at Prince's side. As a first step in auto-iconography the whole thing is awesomely garish. ("Only Prince . . .", you hear yourself muttering.)

For You's music doesn't quite live up to the pretensions of either its cover or its splendid introduction. In fact, much of it is essentially lightweight: the airily innocuous jazz-funk of 'My Love Is Forever', the saccharine Philly-style ballad 'Baby' (which did end up with strings), the token, frantically busy disco outing 'Just As Long As We're Together', and the acoustic, supper-club jazz of 'Crazy You' and 'So Blue'. There is little audacity or innovation to the writing here; Prince is risking nothing, coasting rather on the influences of people like Earth, Wind & Fire. The New York critic Stephen Holden thought the album sounded like "Todd Rundgren singing Smokey Robinson", but actually there's nothing on it as good as Rundgren singing Smokey's 'Ooh Baby Baby' on his 1973 album *A Wizard, A True Star* (which must have influenced Prince). Prince's main object seems to be to impress on us his versatility and multi-instrumental genius. (The dust cover painstakingly lists every instrument he plays on every track.)

But there are definite pointers to the future all the same. For one, the sound is different enough, radical enough, to suggest that an interesting sensibility is at work here. 'Soft And Wet' and 'In Love' particularly work as blueprints for the kind of light, minimalist synthesizer funk to come. "I wanted to make a different-sounding record", he says. "We originally planned to use horns, but it's really hard to sound different if you use the same instruments. I created a different kind of horn section by multi-tracking a synth and some guitar lines." And perhaps more significant still is the thunderous climax to the LP 'I'm Yours', a swirling tornado of heavy metal-on-a-funk-foot that only Earth, Wind & Fire could previously have got away with. Melding Jimi Hendrix, Todd Rundgren and early Van Halen, it is the first clear sign of the rock-funk hybridisation in Prince's *oeuvre*. As a modest first stage in his revolution, *For You* also establishes, however tentatively, the parameters of Prince's "implied naughty sexuality". The title 'Soft And Wet' would really say it all if the song's heavy breathing didn't say even more. On 'In Love', too, the line "I really wanna play in your river" is a typical bit of Prince erotica.

The album gave everyone in Minneapolis a tremendous uplift. "I was so proud I actually stood in line at the record store to get his album", remembers Jimmy Jam. "Not only did he make it out of here but he established a sound which I think a lot of people in Minneapolis were going for, which was a very keyboard-dominated sound. He took it a step further by using keyboards as horns and it was ridiculous to me how good that album was. The *For You* album is fantastic, the idea to just use all synths was unbelievable." Sales-wise it was a disappointment (150–200,000), though 'Soft And Wet', released on 28 June with 'So Blue' on the flip, sold a perfectly respectable 350,000 copies and made No. 12 on the black chart. The second single, 'Just As Long As We're Together', fared much

more poorly, barely scraping the black 100 in November. Perhaps Minneapolis writer Jon Bream put his finger on the problem when he observed to Prince in early 1979 that Warners didn't seem to know whether they should market him as a black, disco or pop artist. But Prince himself knew that this was half the point. "There's not one categorisation that all the tracks can fall into", he said at the time. "Some are funk, some hard rock 'n' roll, and others like 'For You' could be classical. It's like it's hard to classify Earth, Wind & Fire, but you can always tell it's them."

If Prince had proved he could sell a few records, he still hadn't shown Warner Brothers executives that he could cut it live. Back in Minneapolis that autumn, he set about forming a band, with Husney and Levinson placing ads in the local press. Interviewed by a local writer, he announced that he was going to use two keyboard players and lots of synthesizers. "I have to try and create a personality group", he said. "I'm looking forward to performing." In the event André Anderson, by then known as André Cymone, rejoined his schoolboy pal and came in on bass; he'd flown out to California to see Prince working on *For You* and later claimed to have made uncredited contributions to the album. He in turn brought in a white keyboard player called Gayle Chapman. Another old acquaintance, David Rivkin's brother Bobby Z, joined on drums. Formerly the drummer with Minnesotan country-folkie Kevin Odegard, he'd also played with Prince in Pepe Willie's 94 East band.

The advertisements produced the two remaining members. Guitarist Dez Dickerson, survivor of Twin Cities rock outfits Whale Bone, Revolver and Romeo, looked like a prototype Spandex rock pig on Hollywood's Sunset Strip: his Japanese headband image was a decisive factor in Prince's gradual incorporation of hard-rock style. Meanwhile keyboard player Matt Fink (Jewish like Bobby Z) came from stints in local rock bands Zachariah and B.T. Rockets, bringing with him a bizarre new-wave surgeon image and a jerking, Devo-inspired dance style. Visually, the line-up was exactly what Prince had fantasised about for some time: a multi-racial, multi-sexual gang, a new wave Family Stone. "There was a lot of pressure from buddies in other bands not to have white players", he later said. "But I always wanted a band that was black and white. Half the black musicians I knew only listened to one type of music and that wasn't good enough for me." "Prince didn't just want funk players", confirms Lisa Coleman, who was to replace Gayle Chapman in the band a year later. "He had a gift for choosing slightly odd people and making it work in his music."

Rehearsals (in Pepe Willie's basement) were long and arduous from the start; the generalissimo was already in control, drugs were out, and members were heavily reprimanded, if not actually fined, for being late. Finally a date was set for the first live performance Prince had given in almost three years, at North Minneapolis' Capri Theatre in January 1979. "I'll be terrified", the local hero confessed in December. "I find it extremely hard to perform for people."

On the night, they played to a tiny crowd heavily infiltrated by Warner Brothers executives. Dez and Prince, the latter still sporting his Afro hairstyle, wore waistcoats and billowing white shirts. By all accounts the nerves onstage were palpable, but Warners were satisfied.

The boy was a star.

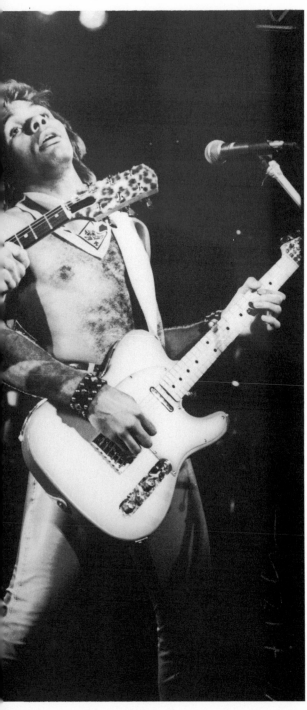

*Prince and Dez
Dickerson in 1980:
"Frederick's of
Hollywood meets the
Rocky Horror Show."*

ROBERT ELLIS

Chapter Three

Black Narcissus

Not long after the Capri Theatre show, Prince broke off with American Artists and found a new manager, Perry Jones, in Los Angeles. No one has ever explained the parting, either from Prince's side or from Owen Husney's. Perhaps Warners simply advised Prince to seek management on the West Coast. Perry Jones didn't last too long either, come to that. A classic Hollywood music-biz type, he was quickly ousted in favour of Bob Marley's old manager, Don Taylor. But Taylor, too, proved unsatisfactory and was soon on his way.

Prince found his current management through a Rhode Island Italian called Steve Fargnoli. With a background in promotion and booking on the East Coast, Fargnoli was brought in by Warners to help get Prince on the road – he'd even worked as Sly Stone's road manager for two years, and was a natural choice to become Prince's agent. When Don Taylor fell through, Fargnoli approached the heavyweight management firm Cavallo & Ruffalo (Earth, Wind & Fire, Ray Parker Jr *et al*) and offered to bring Prince in as a client. Like Fargnoli,

Bob Cavallo and Joe Ruffalo were East Coast Italians. Cavallo had started his career in 1960 by opening a club in Georgetown, the university town adjacent to Washington DC, and by the mid-sixties was managing and producing the hugely successful Lovin' Spoonful in New York, continuing with the group's lead singer, John Sebastian, when they broke up in 1967. With Joe Ruffalo joining as a partner the following year, he signed the brilliant Laura Nyro and oversaw her first Columbia album *Eli And The Thirteenth Confession*. In 1969 they shifted operations to LA, then becoming the real centre of the American rock industry. Over the course of the seventies they managed Little Feat and Weather Report, signing Earth, Wind & Fire in 1972. Ray Parker's career they took over in much the same way they did Prince's, making their move after Parker's group Raydio had hit with 1978's 'Jack And Jill'.

Known in the business as Spaghetti Inc., Cavallo and Ruffalo took Fargnoli on as a partner in the summer of 1979 and made Prince his special responsibility. The various management

43

changes meant that there was a considerable delay before the recording of Prince's second album, and 1979 was for the most part a frustrating year. In the event the record took a mere six weeks to make, "because I knew more about engineering and because I did some demos to prepare for it." Entitled simply *Prince*, it was cut during the early summer at Alfa Studios near the Warner Brothers offices in Burbank – and cut with one thing in mind. "I wanted a hit album", Prince says. "It was for radio rather than for me, and that wasn't the kind of audience I really wanted. They only came around to check you when you had another hit, not when you changed directions and tried something new." In 1982 he told Robert Hilburn of the *Los Angeles Times* that *Prince* was "pretty contrived". It's not really a fair judgement, and one suspects that Prince was once again being wilfully perverse. Indeed, *Prince* is more than just an advance on the terrain staked out in *For You*. It shows the boy maturing as both a soul seducer and a rock funkateer, shows him assuming an array of identities with masterful ease and assurance. With new and highly experienced management at the helm, it represents the true birth of the rude boy genius.

The opening track was 'I Wanna Be Your Lover', released as a single on 22 August. It was Prince's first great song and first real hit, making Number 1 on the black chart and Number 11 pop. Crisp, understated, sinuously lewd, it remains the essence of his early style – a soft priapic strut that enables him to play ambisexual Cupid: "I wanna be your lover/I wanna be your mother and sister too . . ." The riff is compulsively, effortlessly simple, pushing forward his archly camp seduction with irresistible eroticism. "I don't wanna pressure you, baby, but . . ." Here, in this disarmingly boyish flirtation, the falsetto is king: as Ariel Swartley wrote in Boston's *Real Paper* the following March, "falsetto literally confounds sexuality – it's a voice like a woman's coming from a man . . . but it's also a voice like a child's coming from an adult. Prince's home town is in the midst of all the slippery indeterminacies falsetto implies." If he has since borrowed tricks from every great falsetto soul voice – Smokey Robinson, Michael Jackson, Curtis Mayfield, Al Green, the Temptations' Eddie Kendricks – Prince has always achieved an added ambiguity, perhaps even ambivalence. Delivered in this elastic, squealing voice, the line "I wanna be the only one you come for" takes on added kinkiness. As for "I wanna turn you on, turn you out", the latter is a pimp's phrase. This is a choirboy playing Gangster of Love, Shakespeare's Puck on the streets of Harlem.

The cover of *Prince*, released in October, is as ineffably kitsch as its predecessor. If it's true that Prince becomes physically ill in front of the camera, that explains the desperately uncomfortable naked-torso shot on the front. Flip it over and you've got another hilarious example of the boy's auto-iconography: the nude prodigy astride a Pegasus on loan surely from the set of *Clash Of The Titans*. From this garish image of nascent genius to the flasher's raincoat of 1981's *Dirty Mind* is some quantum marketing leap. In fact, though, it makes an obvious but important point about Prince, which is that his narcissism always prevails over both lust and lament. Whatever the context, like Al Green he is invariably making discreet love to himself.

If *For You* swung between the conventional balladry of 'Baby' and the raging guitar lines of 'I'm Yours', *Prince*'s two poles are the hysterical

Prince at the time of Prince: *I wanna be your lover . . .*

headbanger 'Bambi' and the dreamy, doo-woppy 'Still Waiting'. The majority of the tracks fall between these two stools, roughly in the spare mid-tempo vein of 'I Wanna Be Your Lover'. 'Why You Wanna Treat Me So Bad?', the second single off the album, is a bright 4/4 pop-rocker built on Prince's newly patented synth lines and interlaced with some liquid Santana guitar, while 'Sexy Dancer' picks up from the mood of 'I Wanna Be Your Lover', making up for its weak hook with sheer heavy-breathing lewdness. 'When We're Dancing Close And Slow', Side One's closing track, is a slow erotic serenade, building up to a climax on just two slightly sinister chords. "Sex-related fantasy is all my mind can see", Prince warbles, a curiously clinical (but overtly narcissistic) thing to tell someone you're courting.

'With You', the second side's opener, is *Prince*'s 'Baby': a comparatively straight falsetto soul ballad employing safely sentimental chord changes and a gossamer sheen of synthetic strings. The contrast when the churning Hendrix guitar riff of 'Bambi' cranks up couldn't be more extreme. This glam-metal monster concerns a beautiful young lesbian impervious to Prince's charms, but inadvertently it suggests something of his own narcissistic self-absorption: "You had another lover and she looked just like you . . ." (When Prince later had an affair with leading lady Vanity, people made comparisons with Mick and Bianca Jagger. "He said he met his mirror image in me", she said. "That's why he named me Vanity. I was as narcissistic as he was.") Mike Freedberg wrote of the song in the *Boston Phoenix* that "his voice is hysterical, and his masculine self appears only in the crying, hopeless Hendrix-like guitar shrieks. The split ends of his personality do not reconnect, and the song is left an open question . . ."

'Still Waiting', the third single, features Prince at his most playfully heartbroken: there is such exquisite pleasure in the phrasing, in the melismatic whine, that it's difficult to take his pain seriously. More genuinely plaintive is the closing 'It's Gonna Be Lonely', precursor of every classic little-boy-lost Prince ballad from 'Gotta Broken Heart Again' to 'Condition Of The Heart' and not a million miles from the Michael Jackson of 'She's Out Of My Life'. Sandwiched between the two of them is the sprightly 'I Feel For You', deservedly better known in the 1984 hit version by Chaka Khan.

Prince made the boy an official soul star. As Nelson George pointed out six years later in a review of *Parade*, "Well before Prince became a cultural hero and sex symbol, he was just another black teen heart-throb, courting favour with *Right On!* magazine (the black teen bible) and giving puff-piece interviews . . ." (Did anyone imagine in 1979 that this elfin oddball from Minneapolis would go so far?) The period from winter 1979 through to the spring saw Prince giving more interviews than he's subsequently given in eight years; he told Robert Hilburn at the end of 1980 that "I've been spilling my guts out more to the media than I ever have to my friends. They'll find out things from these interviews that they didn't know about!" Even as petrified of the one-on-one interview encounter as he claimed to be – "I think I get more nervous about interviews than I do about being onstage", he said – this is where we begin to see the petulant, childishly enigmatic starlet emerge:

Black Stars: Do you want to be singled out as a certain type of artist – 'efficient' or 'classy'?
Prince: I don't like those two words. 'Scandalous', 'rambunctious', 'obscene' . . .
Black Stars: But you don't appear to be any of those things sitting here.
Prince: Well, I like those – they're more exciting than the other ones.
Black Stars: But are you that?
(He shrugs his shoulders.)

Along with *Black Stars*, Prince talked to the big three – *Right On!*, *Black Beat* and *Rock & Soul* – and put on little performances for each one. Either he'd be completely monosyllabic, catatonic, or he'd be bafflingly ironic. "He often gives the impression", *Black Stars* noted, "of being uninterested or rebellious. He says things – designed to shock, it seems, yet most often just undercutting – to elicit a certain reaction, while his demeanour remains unruffled." The magazines loved it and the little girls, once again, understood.

Prince: You know I don't like to do interviews.
Right On!: But you have to so that people will know who you are.
Prince: Why do they have to know who I am?

The success of 'I Wanna Be Your Lover' also gave Prince added exposure on television, though not always with felicitous results. After appearing on *Soul Train* and Don Kirshner's *Midnight Special* in December, Prince and band were invited on to *American Bandstand*, the biggest TV pop show of them all. Unfortunately, after its famous host Dick Clark made

Arch-enemy Rick James:

"What is most worrying about Prince is that so many people relate to him as a true representative of black America."

the mistake of asking him how he could come from Minneapolis "of all places", Prince became exaggeratedly offhand and sullen – the rude boy had arrived! Rude, again, was the only word to describe his attitude to one Rick James when supporting him on a short tour in the first months of 1980. Pointedly ignoring Rick from the outset, he did everything in his power to upstage him – and usually, by all reports, succeeded. This was the beginning of a long and bitter feud between these arch-rivals in the rock-funk stakes, one that has produced a fair quota of bitchy put-downs from Rick and a slyly amused indifference from Prince. "He is a mentally disturbed young man", Rick was later to say, "but what is most worrying is that so many people relate to him as a true representative of black America. He doesn't even want to be black, and my job is to keep reality over this little science fiction creep." Prince in due course countered by having his giant bodyguard Chick Huntsberry carry him around the auditorium before a James concert in 1984.

Rick was The Sweet to Prince's Marc Bolan. He was glam-funk without George Clinton's satirical vision and wit. Where Parliament-Funkadelic were surreal and subversive, Rick was just trashy and vulgar. And yet he probably exerted more of an influence on Prince than the latter would ever care to admit. Not only did Prince come off the road and immediately begin work on *Dirty Mind*, a DIY masterpiece falling squarely into Rick's "punk-funk" bag, but his later activities as the Svengali of Paisley Park borrowed more than a little from Rick's patronage of artists like Teena Marie and The Stone City Band (his very own Time.) Though by then it sounded suspiciously like sour grapes, Rick later claimed that on the winter 1979–80

47

tour he'd divulged plans to form The Mary Jane Girls, and that Prince had proceeded to steal the concept for Vanity 6.

Prince was at a crucial stage in his development, and live appearances held the key to broadening his audience base. In between dates on the Rick James tour, Prince and band played a series of club headliners that included a show at Minneapolis' Orpheum on 9 February. One of the best of these was at New York's Bottom Line, reviewed by Steve Bloom in the *Soho Weekly News*. "Two problems plagued Prince", Bloom wrote. "The band couldn't really kick out in the limited stage floor-room, nor could the club handle the sheer volume of the sound. Prince belongs in a 15,000-seat arena, rock-style. There's no doubt in my mind that he'll be playing there soon." Prophetic words indeed, though Georgia Christgau in the *Village Voice* found the whole rock fixation oppressive. "I saw the black lead guitarist's tooth solo coming three songs away", she wrote, "right after I noticed his guitar-pick earring." The Orpheum show itself proved a bitter disappointment, somewhat validating Dick Clark's condescending reference to Minneapolis. Only 1,000 local boys and girls turned up at the 2,300-seater theatre, but then only one major Minneapolis radio station had regularly played 'I Wanna Be Your Lover'. So much for local heroes. Undeterred – in front of his father, no less – Prince gave a first public airing of the notorious 'Head', French-kissing Gayle Chapman during an instrumental break. "Shock treatment", the boy king called it. Not long after, Chapman left the band due to religious convictions!

The reaction in Minneapolis was quizzical. The hard-rock elements in the show seemed to be trampling everything else underfoot, and

local writer Jean Rice observed that "a guy who can't decide if he's a Miracle or in a Purple Haze is going to have trouble giving us more than 'moments' of either." Laura Fissinger commented on the "unsureness and the poker faces" which limited "the credibility of his hypersexuality". If Steve Bloom's rock-arena prognosis was correct, there was still trimming to be done and confidence to be bolstered. Prince was going unequivocally for outrage but perhaps he was going too fast. Even the zebra-striped bikini briefs first sported at LA's Roxy a few weeks later suggested a little boy rummaging through his mother's wardrobe rather than the alluring exhibitionist of post-*Dirty Mind* shows. Reactions elsewhere proved that Prince's "shock treatment" was working just fine. "He should have stayed in LA", said one black punter in New Orleans; "we don't like freaks down here." "We were expecting a guy who dressed more like a man", complained a black girl; "he dressed too weird." Prince retorted that people didn't understand his attempt to "bridge the worlds of rock, funk and jazz." "They thought we were gay or freaks, but we're wild and free. It's no holds barred."

"I just don't think about success", Prince stated in February 1980. "It's all just part of the dream factory. If it happens it happens." Disingenuous maybe; but the next few months showed that Prince was willing to take risks that precious few artists in his position would have dared even to contemplate. Coming off the road and settling once again in Minneapolis, his musical direction underwent a radical shift. If the indications were already there in the hybrid rock-soul fusions of *For You* and *Prince*, the songs he now began writing – 'Head' was the first – showed both a significantly increased awareness of new wave

Above: The boy wonder recording demos in Minneapolis, 1977

Right: John L. Nelson with date: "Maybe I'm just like my father, too bold . . ."

Far right: Prince the broken-hearted balladeer – 'How Come U Don't Call Me Anymore?', Detroit, 1984

Right: Prince the guitar hero at London's Lyceum, June 1981
Below: The rude boy pervert of Dirty Mind – "Are you just gonna sit there and watch?"

RETNA

Far right, clockwise: Prince with man-mountain bodyguard Chick Huntsberry; the inner court of The Revolution; Amadeus in lace; André, Prince and Dez, a black Sex Pistols

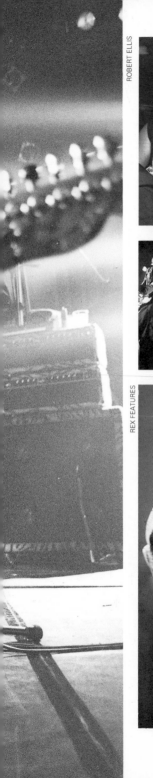

*Left: A second
coming thru Purple
Haze – Prince as
Hendrix
Above: The funk punk
in London, 1981*

rock and a willingness to push his pornographic fantasies as far as they would go. In March he started hanging out at Sam's – rechristened First Avenue a few months later – and hearing records by the likes of Devo, Talking Heads, and the B-52s. On the one hand he heard the three-minute guitar vignettes of the skinny-tie groups – retro power-pop – while on the other he noted the common ground between the synthpop bands and his own use of electronics. As the eight songs of *Dirty Mind* attest, the crude heavy metal which had infused 'I'm Yours' and 'Bambi' was being ousted in favour of something much more compact, minimalist. New Wave Metal Punk-Funk is about as close as I can come to labelling it.

Prince has said that the sound of the 16-track demos which make up *Dirty Mind* had much to do with the "real raggedy" Fender Telecaster guitar he bought before beginning work on them. "My songs depend a lot on what instrument I write on", he says. "When I write on guitar, I come up with songs like 'When You Were Mine' and 'Ronnie Talk To Russia', whereas when I start with drums I get 'Controversy'." Where *Prince* had been written almost exclusively on keyboards, *Dirty Mind*'s songs were mostly written on the new guitar. When it came to recording them, too, "I started to play more on it, rather than just filling in the space with other instruments." It was a sound that marked a profound departure from his sepia teen pin-up status. As he subsequently put it, "I'm not a punk, but I'm not an R&B artist either – because I'm a middle-class kid from Minnesota, which is very much white America." Some have seen *Dirty Mind*, released after an LA remix in October, as a conscious wooing of teenage America's white majority, and if it

isn't that – its X-ratable lyrics had it banned from most radio and some retail outlets, after all – it is still a clear statement of nonconformity, and a refusal to limit himself to black success. When Rick James said that Prince didn't want to be black, he was half-right. "I think society says if you've got a little black in you, then that's what you are", Prince told a *Newsweek* reporter in 1981. "I don't." And after opening for Rick in Fort Worth, Texas, he said "I don't like categories at all. I'm not soul and I'm not jazz, but everyone wants to put one of those labels on me." As Steve Bloom had noted in his *Soho Weekly News* review, "growing up in the heartland (Lord save me if there are ghettoes in Minnesota) will do it to you every time." Indeed, the very fact that Prince played guitar onstage immediately set him apart from the vast majority of young black contenders. Can you imagine *Michael Jackson* with a Fender Telecaster?

Perhaps Mike Freedberg made the most perceptive observation when he reviewed a show at Boston's Paradise Theatre: "[Prince] accomplished what every black rock act seeks to do: to defeat rock on rock's turf and on rock's terms . . . the centre trio entered in punk leather and quickly made the point of black rock: that rock is only a stone until an R&B band turns it into gold, because only black rockers know the alchemy – the suspense of syncopation, the pirouette of boogie vamps, the swing of shuffle playing, the sexual scream of bent notes and guileful chords." We've already noted some of the exemplars of "black rock"; Jimi Hendrix was the outstanding example. Others had tried to forge some kind of alliance between black and white traditions before Prince came on the scene, and still others have built on their foundations since he became a *bona fide* superstar. In an

53

admirably comprehensive article about black rock, New York writer Pablo Guzman traced the parallel developments of white rock and black R & B and noted the various turning points in their relations to one another. "Three major albums were seminal in the new idiom – Stevie Wonder's *Music Of My Mind* (1972), Marvin Gaye's *What's Goin' On* (1971) and Curtis Mayfield's *Live* (1971). These 'concept' albums opened black heads for days, incorporating many forms of late-sixties rock and synthesizing them in new terms. War, Mandrill, Kool & the Gang, Santana and The New Birth were all created in this new form." Contemporaneous, as Guzman notes, was the blistering jazz-rock of Miles Davis' *Bitches' Brew* (1970) and its spin-offs in Weather Report, Herbie Hancock, and The Mahavishnu Orchestra.

The next phase Guzman terms "Funk 'n' Roll". It included George Clinton's groups Funkadelic and Parliament, Earth, Wind & Fire, Cameo, The Gap Band, Mutiny, Zapp, Rick James, Slave, Bootsy and The Brothers Johnson, right up to the hardcore rap and hip hop of the eighties. ('Who Says A Funk Band Can't Play Rock Music?', challenged Clinton on Funkadelic's *One Nation Under A Groove* LP.) These were all acts branching out from the R & B and soul traditions of the fifties and sixties, eclectic aggregations using large horn sections and experimenting with rock ingredients. It was a movement, if such a term can be used, that stretched from the post-Hendrix guitar wizardry of Ernie Isley (of The Isley Brothers) through the Jeff "Skunk" Baxter solo on Donna Summer's 'Hot Stuff' to the incendiary hardcore punk of Washington DC's Bad Brains. It made possible collaborations between Michael Jackson and Eddie Van Halen, between

Run DMC and Aerosmith, and it established a climate in which Prince could make a record like *Dirty Mind*. "Are these black punk acts and New Wavers shunning their traditional black roots in favour of a little cosmic Uncle Tomming", asked *Soul Teen* magazine apropos of Prince and others, "or are they merely climbing over the walls built by the white man and designed to keep black music microcosmic?" It's a question which would have seemed immaterial to Prince, who had long ceased acknowledging the existence of the walls.

Pablo Guzman in his article noted that Prince had "far more readily-identifiable swing with the black audience" than an act like the now-forgotten Bus Boys but that on *Dirty Mind* he "uses far more elements thought to be the sole province of (white) new wave – sparse instrumentation, metallic mix, straight 4/4 drive, neo-decadent lyrics – than the (black) mainstream is currently comfortable with." He went on to make the good point that "the white audience, well-adjusted to theatrical norms of shock by Alice Cooper, Kiss and Bowie, are more ready to look through Prince's sexual ambivalence and stage posturing." Amusingly, though, when Prince is asked in the article if he's in the same league as, say, Devo or The Clash, the mischievous imp sneers, "Maybe, but those guys can't *sing*." A little soul snobbery never did anyone any harm!

Some people weren't so convinced by Prince's disruption of categories at this early stage. "To this taste", wrote John Rockwell in the *New York Times*, "his work seems a calculated, not very original pastiche of several rock styles, of note mostly because of what it says about black attitudes to white rock. If George Clinton, in a visual sense, represents a black extension of late-

"Who Says A Funk Band Can't Play Rock Music?"

George Clinton

sixties acid rock, Prince is essentially a similar equivalent for early-seventies glitter rock, with a bit of punk thrown in for contemporaneity." A harsh verdict, perhaps, but then how many people in early 1980 really saw the boy as much more than a diverting novelty?

Dirty Mind put paid to such scepticism, winning the critics over in droves. As *Spin* magazine later noted, "it sounded like nothing so much as a one-man *Sun Sessions*, and what could make a rock critic happier?" It was an onanist's private party, the sound of a precocious *dauphin* in total, solipsistic control. From the pounding synth-metal opening of the title track to the closing multi-tracked chants of 'Partyup', it was Prince having the ball of his life. "Basically they were demo tapes", he says, "and I had no idea they'd end up as an album. That's where a lot of the upfront quality comes from. I recorded at a lot of small 8- and 16-track studios around Minneapolis – just personal songs I wanted to have. When Steve [Fargnoli] suggested we put them out as the next album, at first I thought it was too much me. It was like an exposé that I wasn't sure I wanted other people to hear. But it was important that I put something out that I liked."

With the wisdom of hindsight, the release of this LP can be seen as a brilliant move. Commercially it looked like suicide, but it established a definitive style and attitude for the "rude" boy that laid a bedrock for the future: "the record company was saying 'Man, you're gonna have the NAACP (National Association for the Advancement of Coloured Peoples) on you', and I said 'Well, so be it'." Prince knew instinctively that this was make-or-break time: that he either risk and go all the way now or turn back for ever. The fact that some of the most

55

conservative reactions to *Dirty Mind* were from black pressure groups didn't faze him. Even *Billboard*'s respected black writer Nelson George charged that 'Head' and 'Sister' were "overt examples of a quite disgusting immaturity" and that "Mr Nelson doesn't seem to understand that wit, understatement and style get one laid much more often than vulgarity." Vulgarity, of course, was part of the essence of Prince's genius. As he well knew, there were quite enough debonair, Marvin Gaye-style ladykillers to go round. Moreover, he didn't quite have the build to be another Teddy Pendergrass. No, this was a rude boy, bastard new wave offspring of the sixties Jamaican hustlers who originally went under that name, and he was tired of understatement. "The lyrics on *Dirty Mind* were straight from the heart", he says, "whereas the earlier albums were more feelings, more dreams and fantasies, and stuck more to the basic formulas I'd learned through playing Top 40 material in Grand Central and Champagne."

The album's cover immediately signalled a minor revolution. No doe-eyed young innocent here, more a lewdly corrupted pixie halfway through a sex change. The accoutrements – the studded trenchcoat, the bandana, the G-string – have clearly been bundled together in the spirit of Oxfam chic, but the face is haunted, provocatively otherworldly. On the reverse, one finds the gang warrior with a broken heart, the style terrorist who needs mothering. The song titles meanwhile are sprayed aggressively on the wall, and the whole monochrome design seems pitched at the glam-rock heavy metal heartland of America. "The jumble", as Laura Fissinger wrote of the band's live image, "is very Minneapolitan in its uncalculated disregard for what, *exactly*, is hip." "Fredericks's of Hollywood

meets The Rocky Horror Show" was another writer's succinct description.

'Dirty Mind' the song is a perfect introduction to the album's preoccupations. From the opening bars the sound is more confidently sexy than anything Prince had previously recorded: essentially rock in approach but fired by funk. 'When You Were Mine' follows and to this day remains one of the greatest songs the man has ever written. It's pure skinny-tie genius, with its arch lyric of jealousy and implicit bisexuality over nervy power-pop guitar and Farfisa organ: "When you were mine/I used to let you wear all my clothes" runs one line; and another reads: "I never was the kind to make a fuss/When he was there, sleeping in between the two of us . . ." It's brilliantly *pervy* while never forsaking the desperate loss of its central hook, "love you more than I did when you were mine". 'Do It All Night' is pretty straightforward, a marvellously spruce and upbeat statement of desire that tumbles rather well into the resignedly blue aftermath of 'Gotta Broken Heart Again'. "The album lacks the sparkling ballads of the previous two", sighed *Blues And Soul*, but this short, sweetly melancholy tailpiece makes up for that. ("I guess I just wasn't in the mood for ballads", Prince responded. "When I did the others, I think I was in love – and I wasn't when I did this one.") The song ends with what sounds like a door being slammed at the end of a long corridor. Perhaps it's just Prince locking up for the night.

The mood of buoyant, strutting confidence resumes on Side Two's opening 'Uptown', a five-and-a-half-minute manifesto of liberation from society's cramping mores and restrictions. This is the first time Prince gives vent to a fantasy of communal release deriving from a personal myth of the sixties: Uptown is almost a nocturnal gateway to the more serene surroundings of Paisley Park, an idealised neon Eden. And this is yet another feather in Prince's eclectic cap, making him a sort of glitter hippie. "People should wake up and not worry about what people think of them", he'd said in February 1980, "like it was in the sixties. People used to go to concerts with their mothers' clothes on and paint all over their faces and it didn't matter. The crowds were wilder than the acts. Now it's all commercial and cool. We'll suffer a slow death like that."

"Where I come from we don't give a damn", Prince yelps on 'Uptown', "we do whatever we please . . . white, black, Puerto Rican, everybody just a-freakin'." It's the boy's very own new-wave Be-In, a Minneapolis version of Bob Marley's Punky Reggae Party. The liberation he espouses is really liberation from cool itself, from the paralysing pressure to be hip: "Owen [Husney] used to tell me a lotta times that when he was growing up there weren't really fads, y'know, musical fads, fashion fads, things like that. People were trying to do something different from the next cat. I guess that's probably how psychedelic music came into being, because everybody was trying to be so out and crazy it just went overboard." Prince's own neopsychedelic phase was a few years off, but already he was fascinated by accounts of events like Woodstock and Monterey and told Andy Schwartz of the *New York Rocker* that he'd always imagined there would be more "spirit" to the music business. Strangely, he never acknowledged the discrepancy between these starry-eyed fantasies of festivity and the fact that he worked entirely alone on his music. For Prince, the fantasy is so much happier than the reality.

On 'Uptown', too, Prince makes a sly reference to the sexual ambiguity of his image:

"What's up little girl/Ain't got time to play/She really didn't say too much 'cept 'are you gay?'/ That took me by surprise, I didn't know what to do/I just looked her in the eyes and said 'no, are you?'" The implication as the verse unfolds is that the girl is such a "victim of society" she can only infer that the liberated Prince must be gay. If she just spent a little time uptown, she too would be freed from her prejudices. Of course the concept of "liberation" is stretched a little further on 'Head' and 'Sister', the next two tracks. Just how the view of womankind expounded in a song like 'Head' tallies with Prince's notions of brotherly love is hard to determine. (It's also hard to square those notions with his claims that he was "hanging out with pimps, prostitutes, and drug dealers" before writing the album: yet more bizarre contradictions.) The sado-masochistic undercurrents in many of his songs may be no more than tongue-in-cheek throwbacks to his early schooling in pornography, but certainly sex is less often about tenderness or indeed freedom in Prince's music than it is about power and submission. The protagonist of 'Head' is a young virgin on her way to be wed. Accosted by Prince at his most sleazily satyr-like, she goes down on him and marries him instead of her fiancé. "Give you head/Till your love is red/Head/Love you till you're dead." Millie Jackson, eat your . . . er, heart out. The music is fabulous, by the way – a grinding funk groove punctuated by lubricious spurts of synth and slap bass. "'Head' was a lot longer", Prince has said. "When I first cut it, it went on and on. I was trying to take a real-life experience. There are parts of the longer version that are sometimes shocking to me."

As for the 90 frenzied soul-punk seconds of 'Sister', well, even seasoned rock 'n' roll animal

57

Dez Dickerson was shocked. "Sex had always been there in the songs", he says, "but it was much more muted at the beginning. I think what really made it become more blatant was the tour we did between the second album and *Dirty Mind*. I divorced myself from the costume side of it – I thought if he wants to go out in a gerbil suit, fine, do it. But I began to feel sex had been overdone in rock 'n' roll in general." (He would later refuse to sing the chorus of 'Sister' in performance.) Actually the song is very funny: "She doesn't wear no underwear", Prince squeals; "she says it only gets in her hair!" Laura Fissinger complained that the song's message – "incest is everything it's said to be!", if it needs spelling out – is "too close to the involuntary sexual abuse that too many children experience", but the sister in question is twice Prince's age.

The final track is 'Partyup', written as legend has it by Prince's old Champagne cohort Morris Day but credited to our hero in return for setting up The Time around Day. It's another irresistible slice of jumping funk, a "protest" anthem about senile politicians who send young groovers like Prince off to war. "It's about this 75-year-old guy who's got one foot in the grave and sipping pina coladas in Palm Springs and he's ready to press the button and start a war that the young people are going to have to fight for him. It's never *his* son . . . oh no, he pays off the right people so that his son doesn't have to go." A superb live number, it ends with the angry, rallying chant: "You're gonna have to fight your own damn war, 'cause we don't wanna fight no more!" What a rebel!

The album was finally released on 15 October 1981, complete with Warner Brothers warning stickers. It was the most uncompromising declaration of intent the rude-boy king could possibly have made.

59

Chapter Four

His Kingdom Come

It is another measure of Prince's internal contradictions that at the time he was making the bold leap forward of *Dirty Mind* he was also suffering an intense depression – one that marked a profound turning point in his whole outlook. Brought on by unrequited love and by a lack of communication within his band ("I couldn't make them understand how great we could be together if we all played our part"), it made him "think differently about how and what I wrote and how I acted towards people" and began the quasi-spiritual journey towards "Paisley Park". "Paisley Park is the only way I can say I got over it now", he said in a *Rolling Stone* interview in 1985. "Paisley Park is the place where one should find oneself, where one can go when one is alone." He added: "It's just so nice to know there is someone and someplace else. And if we're wrong, and I'm wrong, and there is nothing, then big deal! But the whole life I just spent, I at least had some reason to spend it."

It's maddeningly vague, to be sure, but perhaps Prince was tasting the first bitter fruits of his megalomania. And perhaps the band shot on the dust jacket on *Dirty Mind* – a futurist punk gang lined up against a radiator – was his attempt to let others share the spotlight. Certainly the band *in toto* was a pronounced part of the impact his live shows made on audiences all over America in early 1981. Visually arresting with its black front line/white back line tableau, the show was a splendidly *outré* cross between glam-rock blowout and slick soul parade. André Cymone and Dez Dickerson, flanking Prince at the front, looked like a black fusion of Van Halen and The Sex Pistols, with Dez playing the perfect Keith Richards foil to Prince's narcissistic Jagger. At the back, Lisa Coleman dressed as a female sleuth in hat and raincoat while Matt "Dr" Fink perfected his robotic surgeon's dance.

Lisa had joined the band after the religious-minded Gayle Chapman balked at Prince's increasingly explicit sexuality. Lisa was an original rock 'n' roll brat from Los Angeles, daughter of session percussionist Gary Coleman, and a keyboard player since the age of

*Prince and band in
1980: Left to right:
Matt "Dr" Fink, Dez
Dickerson, Bobby "Z"
Rivkin, Prince, André
Cymone, Lisa Coleman*

three. When she heard that Prince was hunting for a replacement for Gayle Chapman, she sent a tape to Steve Fargnoli. Prince loved it. "He wanted to meet to see if I was nice", she says, "so he flew me to Minneapolis and took me to his house. When we got there he sent me downstairs to his studio and told me to start playing. I was kinda nervous since I knew he could hear me upstairs, but then he came down and picked up a guitar and we started to jam. A week later I was living in Minneapolis." She was to become an integral part of the line-up, remaining with Prince another six years.

Prince's confidence onstage had improved dramatically. "I know I don't feel human when I'm up there", he said at this time; "I feel like an animal. If I'm doing a slow number, that's when I'm the closest to the real me, but when I'm doing a fast song and jamming – for it to be effective I must get into the right state of mind for that song. If it's an angry song I must get angry." For someone who'd once found the experience of being a frontman "spooky" he'd come a long way. "It's a real powerful feeling – not the kind of power you have over anyone else but the power that's going on around and through me . . . I think I'm only a conductor of whatever electricity comes from the world, or wherever we all come from."

The major revelation of the gigs played through the new year was the appearance in real numbers of white punters. If *Dirty Mind* lacked a hit single – 'Uptown' made Number 5 on the black chart, but pop success was negligible – critical reception in the rock press was unanimously championing: the *Village Voice* even placed it ninth in its prestigious annual Pazz & Jop poll. On 12 January 1981, Prince's publicist Howard Bloom wrote to Steve Farg-noli: "The verdict from the press is clear: Prince is a rock 'n' roll artist! In fact, the press is saying clearly that Prince is the first black artist with the potential to become a major white audience superstar since Jimi Hendrix . . . so the task is to hold his black audience while aggressively pursuing the rock and New Wave audience." Bloom urged Prince to start doing phone interviews with rock papers around the country, adding that the touring strategy from now on would be critical. "I'd suggest booking him two dates, one in each market: a date as second act on the bill to a major black headliner like Cameo or Parliament and a date at the local New Wave club (Ritz, Emerald City etc.). The white kids who would go to see Prince at the Ritz would never go to the Felt Forum to see Cameo (they're sure they'd be mugged or raped), while the black kids who flock to see Cameo wouldn't think of going to the Ritz."

In fact, just two and a half months later, a healthy mixture of black "uptown flash" and white "downtown trash" converged on New York's Ritz to see the heir apparent come of age, mixing it up in a way that paralleled his own half-calculated, half-innocent jumbling of styles. As Tim Sommer noted in *Sounds*, the blacks (including the likes of Nile Rodgers and Nona Hendryx) were dressed as "sharp punks or upper-class whites", while the whites had kitted up as "lower-class punks or college students." "Is this", Sommer asked, "a funk artist appealing to white middle-American kids weaned on Cheap Trick and Journey, or is it the other way round?" The answer seemed to be a bit of both. It was an extraordinarily assured performance, the meticulously synchronised swaggering of the raincoated front line witty at the same time as it was mildly intimidating. For anyone watching

him for the first time, the spectacle was nothing short of intoxicating. If there was a preponderance of metal guitar antics from Dez and Prince himself, this was admirably offset by both the taut funk of numbers like 'I Wanna Be Your Lover' and the spine-tingling ballad theatrics of 'Gotta Broken Heart Again' and 'It's Gonna Be Lonely'. "It was the most incredible thing I ever saw in my life, and I've seen everybody", gushed Al Kooper, legendary keyboard player and ex-Dylan sideman. "It took me fourteen months to come down from it. I couldn't shut up about it. I was a Prince maniac and nobody wanted to know." This writer returned to England with much the same problem.

The rock establishment's reception of *Dirty Mind* and the live shows was one of the last occasions on which the American press really had any impact on an artist's career. "Can rock critics help an artist sell an additional 100,000 units of an album that had stopped selling?", asked *Record World* in disbelief. Bob Regehr of Warner Bros confirmed that, without the support of black radio, "the album had slowed considerably by the end of 1980", and that sales had picked up in the new year with no additional airplay. The gamble had worked; Prince's audience began to expand almost by word of mouth. "We're just going to keep playing until enough people hear us", he told *New York Rocker* in June.

Not everyone was as unequivocally enthusiastic about the shows. When Prince played London's Lyceum on 2 June – his only British appearance before the great Wembley Arena shows five years later – even a confirmed fan like *NME*'s Ian Penman was troubled by the frequent lapses into rock excess. "Whilst on record the sly Prince can conjure a sexual *mise en scène* in a dizzying matter of minutes and syllables", he

wrote, "in public it's got to be LONGER LOUDER MORE TECHNIQUE . . ." Scorning the comparisons with Jimi Hendrix, Penman protested that Prince's heavy metal "never began to shimmer with a hint of the historical *avant*-shapelessness or spirited slipstreams or sexual harangues" of that master. "This was calculated, coldly choreographed strut rut music, in which context Prince's thigh flashes and camp come-hither persona are stretched pretty thin." To be sure, it was a less satisfying performance than the Ritz, but Penman's verdict was ungenerous: anyone present should have seen the potential of this band. Merely evaluated as a dancer – "he moves like Nijinsky with his ass on fire", as Tony Parsons remarked – the kid was electrifying to behold.

Prancing punks

66

Back in America (the remaining British dates had been cancelled after the disappointing Lyceum turnout) an era of sorts came to an end when André Cymone left the group. It was a split which had been on the cards for some time, both because Cymone wanted to be a star in his own right and because his resentments against Prince were making it impossible for them to work together. In later interviews he was to claim that Prince took credit for one of his songs and taunted him with it; more generally he felt his contributions to the first three albums and to the band's image had been grossly undervalued. He's even claimed that The Time was *his* concept. "I never wanted to be a solo act", he says. "I would have stayed in that group but I enjoy playing in a happy environment with musicians who enjoy playing with each other. And that wasn't the case in Prince's band." Signed to American Artists – Owen Husney quickly scooped up the debris left after the Prince/Time fallout – Cymone has released three unremark-

"Scandalous, rambunctious, obscene . . .": Some of Prince's preferred epithets

The nubile savage in hea[t] Lyceum 1981: reached puberty, I g[ot] new management . . . and I got a new guitar.

able sub-Prince solo albums, *Living In The New Wave*, *Surviving In the 80s* and *André Cymone*. The only success he's had as an artist has been with the Prince-composed 'The Dance Electric'. As a producer, however, following in the footsteps of Prince and Jam & Lewis, he had a Number 1 smash last year with Jody Watley's 'Looking For A New Love'. A co-production with David Rivkin, Prince's original demo producer at Studio 80, it was a shameless pastiche of the Jam & Lewis sound on Janet Jackson's *Control* but a good record nonetheless.

In July, an album appeared on Warner Brothers which bore all the hallmarks of Prince's new Minneapolis sound. The eponymous debut of an entity called The Time, its cover featured six rather studiedly cool dudes posed on the steps of a ghetto tenement, the mascara'd and light-complexioned frontman bearing more than a fleeting resemblance to Prince himself. If you knew nothing about the Minneapolis scene you might have judged there was a possible connection to the miniature maestro; the only clue was that they shared the same management company. If you did know something about it you'd have noticed that the frontman was none other than Morris Day, one-time drummer with Champagne. You might even have guessed that co-producer Jamie Starr was actually Prince – the first of many pseudonyms the purple wonder has employed. Certainly you couldn't have failed to notice the small one's imprint on almost every track: either he was involved or it was a deadly accurate pastiche.

The truth emerged slowly. Initially a story about Prince discovering the band in a Minneapolis bar was concocted, then some astute hack discovered that all the songs had been written by "Jamie Starr" but were owned by "Prince

Rogers Nelson". Finally, Morris Day admitted that even he had scarcely been involved in the project, that essentially this was a bunch of harder-edged, blacker songs that Prince had wanted another outlet for. In return for the use of Morris' song 'Partyup' on *Dirty Mind*, Prince offered to put a band together around him and brought him into the studio to sing lead vocals over six tracks he had once again recorded by himself: 'Get It Up', 'Girl', 'After Hi School', 'Cool', 'Oh, Baby' and 'The Stick'.

From the opening 'Get It Up', one can see why Prince decided to perform this first of many ventriloquist turns. The track is inimitably *Prince* but it's also very strait-laced, a disposable dancefloor strut distinguished solely by its lewd importunings. Prince chirps along in the background and supplies a laboured, sub-Ernie Isley guitar solo, but otherwise it could be any early eighties hack-funk combo. The ballad 'Girl', likewise, could have come from *For You* or *Prince* but not from *Dirty Mind* – a pretty enough tune but hardly another 'Gotta Broken Heart Again'. As for 'After Hi School', a flimsy piece of bubblegum power-pop, it would be unworthy of Vanity 6 let alone of Prince. The album's one triumph is 'Cool', a ten-minute flexing of Day's braggadocio that's brilliantly undercut by its bittersweet melody. 'Oh, Baby' isn't bad, it must be said – a typical piece of Prince seduction that manages to sound forlorn even as it croons sweet lust, with the master's falsetto winding sinuously round Morris' moans. 'The Stick', finally, is the first of the dance opuses (viz. 'The Walk', 'The Bird') that became such centrepieces of The Time's live show.

With the album finished and sent off to Warners for their reaction, the immediate task

The Time, *1981:*
(Clockwise from left)
Terry Lewis, Jimmy
Jam, Jellybean Johnson,
Monte Moir,
Jesse Johnson and
Morris Day

in hand was putting a band together and grooming it. Thus was Prince the Svengali, the enlightened despot, born – a character at once generous and dominating. "You can't work with Prince unless he controls you absolutely", says Alexander O'Neal, whom Prince had originally wanted to build The Time around. The musicians Prince did eventually recruit came in fact from Flyte Tyme, the group O'Neal fronted and old rivals from Champagne days. Newer additions to the band's original nucleus of bassist Terry Lewis and drummer Jellybean Johnson were keyboard man Jimmy Jam (ex-Mind Over Matter) and guitarist Jesse Johnson (ex-Enterprise and Band Of Pleasure). Together with white keyboard player Monte Moir (for that token multi-racial touch?), this foursome became The Time – although their contributions to the album extended only to posing in new-wave gangster togs on the cover. "They dress with the studied arrogance of middle-class punks", wrote Vernon Gibbs in the *Village Voice*, "whereas bands who escape from the inner city are usually much more eager to get into lavender sequin tights."

While the album duly went gold, outselling *Dirty Mind* in six months, Prince drilled the group with the same remorseless pressure he'd applied to his own musicians. "He would give us keyboard parts that were impossible", remembers Jimmy Jam. "We would be like, 'we can't play these'. He would be like, 'yeah you can, and while you're playing them I want you to do this step of choreography and sing this note of harmony.' Couple of days later we'd be doing it. A month later we'd be on tour and it would be automatic. We watch tapes of those shows and you look back and say damn, I did *that*. He was a great motivator and the thing that made him a

great motivator was that he works so hard himself. He's always squeezing the most out of everything." "We were able to avoid making a lot of mistakes", adds Morris Day, "because Prince had already made them and passed his knowledge down to us. We had one common goal and that was to be the first to the top. From that attitude everything else started to click personality-wise. That cohesion you saw onstage came from our motivation and twelve-hour-a-day rehearsal schedules."

With The Time off and running, then, Prince adjourned to LA to begin work on his own next album. Released at the beginning of October, it was titled *Controversy* and featured on its cover a dandified, over-made-up version of the *Dirty Mind* character. Naff isn't the word for this beauty: a wing collar and bootlace tie under a studded mauve trenchcoat do not a sharp-looking motherfucker make. As for the livid orange complexion, something has gone seriously askew in the airbrushing department. *Controversy* doesn't work because it suffers from delusions of grandeur. In saying "I am controversial" – the wild and liberated Eros who made that naughty *Dirty Mind* LP – Prince opens himself up to ridicule. As a self-conscious postscript to the "scandal" of its predecessor it loses all the spontaneous power of that record. "Controversy is press" had been one of Owen Husney's catchphrases, but here the principle is applied with a crude lack of irony. Not only is the theme of "controversy" tied to the aftermath of *Dirty Mind* – "I just can't believe all the things people say/Controversy/Am I black or white, am I straight or gay?" – but it's used as a pretext for Prince to sound off pompously on several other matters. Yes, the album says, I'm going to be *even more* controversial. If 'Uptown'

and 'Partyup' hinted at the mini-demagogue inside him, 'Sexuality', 'Ronnie Talk To Russia' and 'Annie Christian' show Prince clumsily ramming home the point that this is no ordinary soul star, that this boy is a real "artist" with real statements up his sleeve. "Some complained about Prince waving all these freak-flag protest slogans in their faces", wrote Richard Riegel in *Creem*. "They wanted more of his magic wand." Well yes, but maybe they just wanted something authentic.

'Controversy', which as a single made Number 3 on the black chart but only Number 70 pop, is seven minutes of robotic new wave funk and one of the most self-preening pieces of music ever recorded. The most controversial thing about it is its spoken insertion of the Lord's Prayer halfway through. Towards the end it comes up with its own pat litany: "People call me rude/I wish we all were nude/I wish there was no black or white/I wish there were no rules." This is really Prince pandering to his own woolly liberal propagandists: one rather earnest Warners press release, for example, opined that "behind the frequently shocking lyrics is a deep belief that by removing the taboos and allowing youth to express its sexuality in all its forms we will achieve a more wholesome society." Wilhelm Reich eat your orgone box out. Only the line "Some people want to die/so they can be free" sound genuinely Princean.

More on "allowing youth to express its sexuality" can be found in 'Sexuality' itself, a trite manifesto saved only by its insistently funky guitar riff. 'Sexuality is all you'll ever need' is the essential thrust of the song's argument. "Sexuality – let your body be free!" Jumping along on a new wave dance-rock bass line it sounds tailor-made for ritzy Hollywood discos;

71

even Prince's pseudo-militant rap about the "new breed" standing up against the anti-sex tyranny of the previous generation fails to lend it any semblance of real soul power. Only in the side's closing 'Do Me Baby', an eight-minute slow-burn of ecstatic falsetto foreplay, does an authentic Prince emerge from the closet of "controversial" cant. Later covered in a fabulous version by Meli'sa Morgan, the song picks up where 'I Wanna Be Your Lover' left off, pinning down its object of desire with waves of lewdly seraphic supplication. "Sex is his shrine", wrote Ian Penman in a review of the album, "and that's where his confusing charm works best." 'Do Me Baby', he noted, is "Smokey Robinson singing obscene moonbeans – lust imploring love . . ." Smokey is the right reference, Smokey and perhaps a kinky choirboy version of Al Green: when the track breaks down into Barry White satin-sheets orgasm the falsetto keeps him from oafish male grunts. In fact it sounds more like a girl coming. Mike Freedberg said that Prince, like Smokey, "uses his falsetto as a sexual mask; as a way to demonstrate to his intended lover that he understands her fears and desires as if he were female himself." And ultimately, of course, there's the now-familiar sense that Prince is actually making love to himself, inviting us to play the voyeur. "Are you just gonna sit there and watch?", he inquires halfway through the song . . .

The simplicity and sensuality of 'Do Me Baby' stand out on an album characterised otherwise by pretentious overreaching. Prince seems to have been angry at people typecasting him as a porn merchant and much of *Controversy* sounds like an anxious attempt to dispel that image. Roy Carr wrote that the boy "would shortchange

himself if, like Alice Cooper, he allowed the media to embrace him and defuse his subversiveness by adopting him as the token friendly neighbourhood pervert" and Prince seems intuitively to have known this. One of the principal reasons he stopped giving interviews was that he felt the press wasn't taking him seriously. "More than my songs have to do with sex", he protested in June 1981, "they have to do with one human's love for another, which goes deeper than anything political that anybody could possibly write about. The need for love, the need for sexuality, basic freedom, equality . . . I'm afraid these things don't necessarily come out. I think my problem is that my attitude's so sexual that it overshadows anything else. I might not be mature enough as a writer to bring it all out yet."

If 'Do Me Baby' suggests delirious self-love, Side Two's opening 'Private Joy' sounds positively masturbatory. This is a camp Prince pouting sweet nothings to the "pretty toy" no one else knows about, a Prince playing with himself in no uncertain terms. It's a witty song, bouncing along on a good-humoured keyboard riff: "I strangled Valentino, you been mine ever since", the prancing cupid sneers. "If anybody asks you, you belong to Prince!" Next up is the two-minute embarrassment of 'Ronnie Talk To Russia', a confused and confusing rant whose lyric is barely discernible through the fog of glam-punk guitars and machine-gun drums. 'Let's Work' is better but remains little more than a pale reprise of the riff from 'Head'. 'Annie Christian' is the worst of the lot, a ludicrous kind of rap allegory about the Antichrist killing John Lennon and the Atlanta children. "Annie Christian, Antichrist/Until you're crucified/I'll live my life in taxi cabs", Prince sings over a dreadfully limp guitar figure and drum machine programme. The logic is far from obvious. At least the closing 'Jack U Off' rounds out the album in a merry spirit. An insubstantial piece of electro-rockabilly trash, it anticipates both 'Delirious' and 'Horny Toad'.

Controversy showed Prince in a state of flux and transition, an artist feeling his way through to the greater confidence of *1999*. "Clearly he is very much a self-creation", Vince Aletti concluded in a *Village Voice* review, "a true rock 'n' roll eccentric with a look, an attitude and a philosophy. Since he's only 21, the persona hasn't been clamped on tight yet, and there's time to be foolish and vulnerable and really surprising." If it remains arguably the man's worst album, it was nonetheless a necessary stage in his growth as both a writer and a performer.

The album misfired as a consolidation of *Dirty Mind*'s critical crossover success. The title track single received scant white airplay, and by the time the tour reached San Francisco's Civic Theatre on Valentine's Day 1982 the audiences were almost entirely black. A week after the LP's release in the first week of October, a golden opportunity to convert some of rock's white majority came when The Rolling Stones squeezed him on to the bill at their Memorial Coliseum shows in LA. It was not a happy occasion. Opening the show under George Thorogood and The J. Geils Band – both, like the Stones, heavily black-influenced rock acts – Prince went down like a lead balloon. "Some dimwits near the front of the stage hurled paper cups and a bottle", wrote the *LA Times*' Robert Hilburn of the Orange County rednecks who doubtless made up a large proportion of the audience. Flying home to Minneapolis, Prince had to be persuaded back by promoter Bill Graham (and some say Mick Jagger himself) to play the second show on Sunday the 11th. Unfortunately the audience this time was even more hostile, and when somebody threw a bag of chicken parts at Prince he stormed off the stage. Bill Graham remonstrated with the crowd but it made no difference. Prince later recounted how he "saw this one guy with hatred all over his face" and had to leave because "I wanted to fight with him". It's probably small consolation to Prince that some of these nerds must later have bought *Purple Rain*.

If *Controversy* sold more than any of his previous three albums, making Number 3 on the black chart and going gold in three months, doubtless it was mortifying to Prince that *The Time* almost did better. Certainly 'Cool' was one of *the* American anthems of summer '81, and many felt the band upstaged their mentor on the *Controversy* tour. Any rivalry, though, was forgotten when the two acts returned in triumph to Minneapolis' First Avenue in March. By now the place had become a kind of clubhouse for Prince and his acolytes, and the gigs gave him his first concrete sense of local acceptance. It was good to be home, too – back in the boring Midwestern city where he could be anonymous for a few months. "I'm kind of an introvert", he told one reporter, "and LA is for extroverts. Every time I have to go there I just dread it. It's that attitude of everybody – I lose sight of what I'm doing when I'm there." That spring he bought the suburban two-storey mansion where he lives to this day, in due course painting it the *de rigueur* purple.

Over the course of the summer Prince began work on the songs which would make up the double album *1999*. It was a tremendously fertile few months, a period in which his whole approach to sound changed radically. "He can't

73

stop working", Lisa Coleman has said. "He'll go to bed at night and get up fifteen minutes later with an idea. He'll call someone or go into the studio and sing a song. He has to find an outlet. We'll be asleep and get a call at 1.30 in the morning saying come to the studio." "The thing is", Prince says, "when you're called, you're called, you know. I hear things in my sleep. I walk around and I go into the bathroom and try to brush my teeth, and all of a sudden the tooth-brush will start vibrating. That's a groove, you know, and you got to go with that. That means drop the toothbrush and get down to the studio, get to a bass guitar quick. I don't know, my best things just come out like that." (Patti "Apollo-nia" Kotero recalls watching Prince in the studio and says it was as if he was "in his own spaceship, his own capsule, just taking off . . .") Estimates on the number of songs stashed away in Prince's vaults vary from 300 to 500, a prolific output which goes a long way to explaining why he releases albums in such rapid succession. The songs on the recent so-called "black" album (as yet unreleased) have almost all been knocking around for two or three years.

"Where most producers do all the rhythm tracks for an album first", Prince says of his working methods, "I like to take each song as its own project. I go into the studio at very strange hours sometimes and do marathon sessions until I'm ready to drop." With the *1999* songs, synthesizers took on an added prominence. "I like synthesizers", Prince had once said; "I don't like horns very much because you can't bend notes on them like you can on a synthesizer." Now he took his new-wave funk sound into another dimension, creating a synthetic soundscape that in critic Robert Palmer's words conjured the image of "glaciers scraping against

Prince with Vanity, 1983:

"He said he met his mirror image in me . . . I was as narcissistic as he was."

each other." One exposure to the icily massive drive of '1999' should be enough to confirm this. The synth drums are huge bottomless throbs, the keyboards surge like a river about to break its banks and only Prince's frenetic, chattering guitar inserts a busy humanness into the computerised pounding. Not that the new sound was robotic: unlike so much dancefloor production in the eighties Prince has never sacrificed emotion or sensuality to the dictates of the beat. But *1999* showed him taking on the English "futurists", for example, and making them look like the effete clotheshorses they were. The Minneapolis sound was defined at last. "Around here, if it's not synthesizers it's nothing", said a local musician in 1983. "This is a keyboard town. It's *simplicity*. If you listen to a lot of Prince or The Time, it's simple. It's direct and straight to the point. And it feels so good."

1999 was far from being a wholly satisfying work – for the most part it sounded like a bunch of half-formed ideas stretched too thin. But it served as a kind of coronation, a ceremony of grandiose self-love. 'Dance Music Sex Romance' was a catechism for the new reign and '1999' was its anthem. "By *1999* things had changed on a number of levels", says Dez Dickerson, who left the band after the gruelling six-month tour that began in October '82. "It was becoming Prince and his band. The philosophies were changing, he was doing brasher things and going out on a limb lyrically. His image was becoming more flamboyant, too. The raincoat went from plain grey to purple – that whole purple thing started. It smacked of a movement and I didn't want to be involved in a movement. We argued many times during that tour, but they weren't arguments in the negative sense, more like debates. I suddenly realized the

band we were in 1981/2 was not the band we were in 1983. It had become very slick and comfortable. No one's ever been able to say no to Prince, but I always spoke my mind and I think he respected me for that."

If on *1999* he avoided the gauche posturings of *Controversy*, still one had the impression of someone who could no longer be satisfied with merely writing good songs. For starters, the eleven tracks averaged six minutes apiece. "I didn't want to do a double album", Prince claimed, "but I just kept writing and I'm not one for editing . . ." For seconds there were all kinds of whimsical self-indulgences which simply didn't come off – the six minutes of 'All The Critics Love U In New York' were only the most obvious example. And for thirds 'Automatic' and 'Let's Pretend We're Married' were just too white by half. Only the very funky, faintly disturbing 'Lady Cab Driver' and the sole slow number 'International Lover' could stand with '1999' or 'Little Red Corvette', the inspired crossover single that finally propelled Prince into pop's first division.

"Sex is no manifesto, no saviour, and certainly no shock", wrote Julie Burchill in an *NME* review of the album. "As my colleague Confucius likes to say, 'Nothing sadder than a flasher whom no one notices'." But *1999* turned out to be a classic "sleeper" of a record, picking up sales after relentless touring had kindled interest from the grassroots up. By the time that tour ended in April 1983, 'Little Red Corvette' had made both MTV and the American Top Ten and Prince had made the cover of *Rolling Stone*. The "flasher" had been noticed.

The tour took the old-fashioned form of a revue, climaxing in Prince's hi-tech purple apocalypse after sets by The Time and a new act called Vanity 6. Consisting of three girls, each symbolising a different aspect of tarty female sexuality, Vanity 6 were Prince's cartoon sex bombs. "We'd all met Prince individually at different times and places", says the group's Brenda Bennett, wife of Prince's lighting director, "and we'd each given him a demo tape. He turned them over to his management and someone there came up with the idea of seeing if the three of us could work together." Brenda hailed from Boston, where she'd sung in a local band called Tombstone, while 19-year-old Dee Dee Winters (Vanity) was a model from Niagara Falls in Canada. (Said Rick James, a native of the area who'd known her previously, "she gave him pussy and he gave her a record.") Only 16-year-old Susan Moonsie, the virgin in white suspenders, came from Minneapolis itself. As a concept it was tackier than Rick James himself: originally they were to be known as The Hookers, with Dee Dee tastefully christened Vagina. Nor did their happy compliance in the concept alter the fact that it probably said more about Prince's attitude to women than he intended.

Ultimately it was harmless enough. As Vince Aletti wrote of the *Vanity 6* album released before the tour, "even when they're oozing 'I need seven inches or more' or going on about wet dreams, it's difficult to take them seriously; they sound like a slightly perverted Shangri-Las – and they reach the same level of delightful pop inanity." A perverted Shangri-Las was exactly what they were – or more exactly, Prince's Ronettes, with Prince playing Phil Spector to Vanity's Ronnie. Songs like 'Nasty Girl' and 'He's So Dull' were cheap, trashy vignettes of vixenish sexuality – "perfect fixes", as Aletti noted, "on a 'little nasty world' of girls and boys

on the make." How much of *Vanity 6* was the work of the little generalissimo is uncertain. More than one of the songs were written by The Time, who had their own album, *What Time Is It?*, out in August. *Sounds* saw *Vanity 6* as "a logical extension of Prince's feminine side", while Carol Cooper suggested the girls were a "triple fracture of Prince's own feminine projections: Vanity, a creamy sort of black Barbarella sandwiched between a sweet, underage brown vixen and a tall, butch blonde who talks like the black Boston ghetto."

What Time Is It? meanwhile was a bold stride forward for Prince's original protégés, building brilliantly on the ideas and attitudes of their debut. "Another Starr Production", says the album sleeve, but how much input Prince had in the project is again difficult to determine. Two of the best songs, '777-9311' and 'Gigolos Get Lonely Too', are Morris Day originals, while the rest of them are credited to The Time (a name, incidentally, owned by Prince). Publisher of all six is Tionna Music, "the sole proprietorship", according to the Library of Congress copyright office, "of author Jamie Starr". Whoever wrote it, the album is great, the sound far stronger and funkier than on *The Time*. If the backstage groupie scenario of 'Wild And Loose' makes the point that this is still an *idea* of a group, a conceptual spoof that produced some hits almost by mistake, there is the real sense here of a band seizing its sound and identity with compelling self-assurance.

The uptempo cuts – especially 'Wild And Loose', '777-9311' and 'The Walk' – are as good as any funk ever recorded, and the smoochy 'Gigolos Get Lonely Too' is as delicious as Prince's 'Gotta Broken Heart Again'. (Given the fabulous songs subsequently written by

Jimmy Jam and Terry Lewis, it's hard to believe that this pair didn't at least have a hand in most of the tracks.) Image-wise, too, the band had patented a perfect look: *Billboard*'s Cary Baker called it "a happenchance combination of new wave, gangster and miscellaneous camp." "I can't pinpoint an era", Morris Day himself said when the tour was almost through. "I like baggy pants but I wear a lot of new stuff, old stuff, and mix it all up." If the marcelled hair-do and eyeliner came from Little Richard via Prince, the vaguely zoot-suit *schmutter* was probably influenced by August Darnell's Original Savannah Band. It was the perfect get-up for Morris' foplike struttings – the camp, new-wave-vaudeville ladykiller.

Actually, The Time made it clear that they were pretty down on new wave. "We don't like new wave!", they bawled in unison at the end of Side One – as if making the heavy-handed point that this was Prince's R & B outlet. But the keyboards and overall sound were more "noowave" than they could have admitted, of course. Like Prince they were branching out from a funk/soul base and incorporating the camp theatrics of much white rock. Indeed, so delightful was their theatre of dance and comic mime on the *1999* tour that they once again blew the headliner offstage every night. Prince himself knew this, even admitting four years later that "they were the only band I was afraid of, and they were turning into, like Godzilla." The little Dr Funkenstein had created a monster he couldn't control, and by the time the tour reached New York's Radio City Music Hall in March, The Time had been demoted to backing Vanity 6 behind a curtain. By then, too, Jimmy Jam and Terry Lewis had left the group, sacked by Prince for missing a show in San Antonio

when they got stranded in a snowbound Atlanta. Like other people who've worked with him, Jimmy and Terry were tired of living under Prince's thumb and had begun touting themselves around as producers. When the snow struck Atlanta they were doing a between-gigs session on The S.O.S. Band.

If the tour was occasionally marred by such acrimonious hiccoughs, it nonetheless signalled the real arrival of Prince and his court. Not only did the exhaustive itinerary pay off in album sales (4 million), but the show worked as a display of Prince's power – this was a mobile empire in the making. Like Tamla Motown's Berry Gordy, Prince had emerged from a Midwestern base and single-handedly put a scene on the map, grooming and styling two acts in a manner that directly recalled Gordy's "quality control panel". "The bands that come under his rule dress just the way he wishes them to", commented *Spin*, "sluttish Barbies and Kens strutting through the purple satin fantasies of a single very inventive adolescent."

His kingdom come, his will was done.

Chapter Five

The Colour Purple

The closest this writer has come to Prince and his circus was during the latter stages of the *1999* tour. Flown from Los Angeles to the nondescript town of Kalamazoo, Michigan, I stayed with the tour until it reached the next date in hometown Minneapolis, and in that 72-hour period formed impressions of Prince's world which have remained with me ever since, impressions on the one hand of the man's extreme remoteness and mystique, on the other of the happy family spirit in that travelling company of friendly perverts. ("We were all like little kids playing a big game", says Jill Jones, who sang back-up for Prince as a peroxide teenager.) Within an hour or so of my arrival, Steve Fargnoli had introduced me to virtually everyone involved in the tour, and almost without exception they were warm and welcoming. Only Prince, of course, was less than delighted when his manager brought a journalist to the door of his dressing room. If the door at least opened, the alarmed and suspicious little face that peeped out and surveyed me hardly made us friends for life.

Every time our eyes met from then on, I felt intensely scrutinised, as if this alien creature sensed that my mission was somehow to *expose it*. By that point in the tour – February 1983 – Prince was rarely seen except in the shadow of his new bodyguard Chick Huntsberry, a 6′ 6″, 300lb beast so fearsome that his previous employers even included Mr T. As a pair, Prince and he looked grotesque and scarcely ever fraternised with anyone else on the tour. When, after the Kalamazoo show, the three principal tour buses pulled into an Indiana truckstop for a slap-up feed, Prince and his minder ate alone in a corner. More curiously still, Vanity, with whom Prince was supposed to be having a passionate love affair, never once spoke to him and remained on the Vanity 6 bus at all times.

"Fargnoli tells me the racial mix of the tour's audiences has varied from town to town", I wrote in the 2 April issue of *New Musical Express*. "Kalamazoo's turnout is predominantly black, and while the girls are Janet Jackson clones, all the young dudes are spruced up like they're understudying for The Time. Whatever else he's up to, Morris Day unquestionably has his dandy finger on a new pulse of black chic. As an aperitif he's the perfect foil for Prince, pretending to no more than poise. His cards are on the table with his gigolo handkerchief and cufflinks, and right now The Time's lack of pretence is paying higher musical dividends than *1999*. Try to imagine Prince as gigolo and the contrast is clear. However sexy he is, Prince is always the little boy lost. The question is, lost in what? If Mike Freedberg could write so perceptively in 1980 that Prince's vulgarity is 'only innocence's parody of cynicism', that innocence is now complicated by a certain grandiosity. It's no longer enough to say that Prince is a choirboy playing Casanova – we've asked him to embody more of pop's contradictions than that. And the more we demand of him, the less he seems able to supply."

I found myself troubled by the new Prince, the purple messiah in his hi-tech lair of ladders and fire poles, chrome blinds and steel catwalks. (Reminiscent of David Bowie's 1978 stage set, in one sense it was the perfect cage-like playground for this bizarre figure.) "What was once irresistibly mincing and charmingly gauche", I noted, " – the clash of styles, rude boy/heavy metal/dirty old new romantic – has turned into an hysterical exhibitionism, Michael Jackson's nervous androgyny filtered through the cocksure vanity of an Adam Ant. The sex is shorn of its erotic charge and plunged into pornography. As 'Little Red Corvette' has it, 'a body like yours ought to be in jail/Coz it's on the verge of being obscene'." It seemed that Prince was getting too big for his six-inch heels: with only those 1981 gigs to compare it to, the *1999* show was like watching the overblown theatre of

Queen after the primal sex explosion of the young Elvis Presley. Overkill ruled. "The machine quakes with its excessive load", I lamented, "and futurism regresses to pomp rock. Far from the tight punch of *Dirty Mind*, this sonic blanket is pumped up with the aural equivalent of silicon. The audience looks bewildered. The tension between Prince's bashfulness and his self-preening no longer holds."

Back in California, I tried to piece together my doubts and disappointments: "The more I read of the boy's raw sex/pure energy politics, the less convinced I am. And yet, the more haze is stirred up around it, the more Prince seems to hide behind it. This nubile savage has become our puppet: the whizzkid-as-prophet. I did not seriously expect to make Prince's acquaintance for the very good reason that Prince does not exist. He avoids me because he is a void. Let's be clear: Prince is not *my* fantasy, he is all of ours. We project him like a holograph. He is where all the desires of pop meet and tangle – their camp cupidon, their locus of signification . . ." My disappointment really came down to this: that Prince was trying to be something that he wasn't, something he thought we wanted him to be. The pure, self-generated abandon of his original incarnation was now tainted by an insidious knowingness. "They won't say that you're naïve", he smarmed on 'All The Critics Love U', "if you play what you believe."

Five years on from my brief on-the-road encounter with His Purpleness ("Prince really identifies with the colour", said *Purple Rain* writer William Blinn; "there's a whole dark, passionate, foreboding quality to it . . ."), I think I can see that the *1999* show was as necessary a stage in his growth as anything he's done,

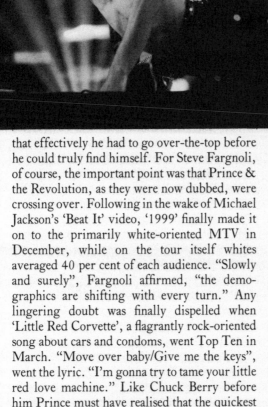

that effectively he had to go over-the-top before he could truly find himself. For Steve Fargnoli, of course, the important point was that Prince & the Revolution, as they were now dubbed, were crossing over. Following in the wake of Michael Jackson's 'Beat It' video, '1999' finally made it on to the primarily white-oriented MTV in December, while on the tour itself whites averaged 40 per cent of each audience. "Slowly and surely", Fargnoli affirmed, "the demographics are shifting with every turn." Any lingering doubt was finally dispelled when 'Little Red Corvette', a flagrantly rock-oriented song about cars and condoms, went Top Ten in March. "Move over baby/Give me the keys", went the lyric. "I'm gonna try to tame your little red love machine." Like Chuck Berry before him Prince must have realised that the quickest way to the heart of the Great White Heartland was via the Great American Automobile. In fact the record did better on the pop chart than on the black one.

If *1999* was clearly overshadowed by the freakish success of Michael Jackson's *Thriller*, it still made Number 9 on the pop album chart, produced two more Top 20 hits in 'Delirious' and the re-released title track, and made clear that in the long term Jacko might have some serious competition on his hands. "Just don't compare me to Michael Jackson", Prince had sneered in 1981, and few would have guessed there'd ever be a need. Now, however, it looked as if Prince could be playing The Rolling Stones to Michael's more wholesome Beatles. (As Marek Kohn observed, "where Jackson is an enchanter, Prince is a card sharp . . ." Four years later, Quincy Jones brought the two black pop gods together in hopes of scaring Michael into finishing *Bad*.)

The rock press was once again in love with

Prince. Despite *Thriller*, *Rolling Stone* voted him 1982's Artist Of The Year, then put him on the cover in March with a portrait by the legendary Richard Avedon. The story inside wasn't even based on an interview: after Robert Hilburn's December piece in the *LA Times*, Prince vowed he would never speak to the press again. "The young singer's doleful eyes suggested the sad resignation of a fugitive cornered after a chase", Hilburn noted, and all remaining interviews, including this writer's, were cancelled.

Besides Chick Huntsberry, a constant companion of Prince's on the *1999* tour was a small notebook – inevitably purple – in which he was often to be seen scribbling. Unbeknownest to most of the tour personnel he was sketching out ideas for a semi-autobiographical film that he'd discussed with Steve Fargnoli, and even The Revolution were still in the dark when a Hollywood writer called William Blinn suddenly showed up for the last leg of the tour. Prince enjoyed the secret, letting them assume he was simply a journalist on an assignment. In fact Blinn was an executive producer of the TV series *Fame* and had won Emmy awards for *Brian's Song* and an episode of Alex Haley's *Roots*. By the end of the tour he had not only a rough idea for a screenplay (tentatively entitled *Dreams*), but some fairly shrewd insights into Prince himself. Noting his "strange mixture of shyness and theatricality", he remarked that Prince seemed to be "sorting out his own mystery" with the film. "It's an honest quest to figure himself out. He saved all the money on shrinks and put it in the movie." Blinn found it hard to communicate with Prince: "He's not purposefully face-to-the-wall, but casual conversation is not what he's good at. He talks in images a great deal, and after you've listened to

him for a while you start to understand that there's a consistency to what he's talking about. He's an enigma. He wants to communicate but he doesn't want you to get too close." "Music", he concluded, "is a cloak and a shield – a womb."

When the tour had finished, and Prince was back in Minneapolis, a 31-year-old University of Southern California film graduate called Albert Magnoli flew into town to discuss the possibility of directing the film. "The *Rolling Stone* story had given me an intuitive sense of Prince and his world", Magnoli recalled. "To me, Prince and The Time's entire thing was visual. The microcosm they'd developed was a movie begging to be made. You listen to '1999' and you picture the opening of an epic." Like Cavallo, Ruffalo & Fargnoli, Magnoli felt that the traditional concert film had been outmoded by the mini-dramas of rock videos and that something closer to the hugely successful *Flashdance* or even *Saturday Night Fever* was needed. "I had no interest in mimicking the past rock 'n' roll films. My idea was to focus on the character's motivations offstage, so that when he did perform there was a hell of a good reason to be there." Staying in Minneapolis for a month, he gathered ideas and impressions of the many characters who inhabited Prince's curious little world, remarking later that "the people in the film are extensions of the personalities of Prince, Morris and company . . . exaggerations or minimisations developed to fit a story that never happened, yet in a strange way *is* their reality."

The key to what made *Purple Rain* work was its DIY feel – the sense that this was a homemade homage to a Minneapolis scene still in the process of forming – and one of the crucial factors in that feel was the decision Cavallo, Ruffalo & Fargnoli made to bypass the usual

*Left: The psychedelic
dandy at the height
of Purple Rain fever*

*Below: Sur la Côte
d'Azur, filming
Under The Cherry Moon*

REX FEATURES

REX FEATURES

*Above: On the set of
Cherry Moon. "Who
tells the truth to a
star?" asked Steven
Berkoff*

Left: The soul showman at New York's Madison Square Gardens, August 1986. The Parade tour revealed him as a true master of ceremony.

Above: Arriving for the Wembley Arena shows, Heathrow

Left: Don't make those Charlie Chaplin eyes at me . . . Wembley 1986

Above: Crucified by desire at Madison Square Gardens

Right: Prince by Fluck and Law

*Clockwise from top
left: A camp James
Brown with "dancing
security" goons
Jerome Benton, Greg
Brooks and Wally
Safford; on the
Sign 'O' The Times
European tour with
Mico Weaver and
Seacer; in take-off
mode with Eric Leeds;
leaving Heathrow
after the Wembley
shows*

For You (1978)

Prince (1979)

Dirty Mind (1980)

Controversy (1981)

1999 (1982)

Purple Rain (1984)

*Around The
World In A Day
(1985)*

Parade (1986)

*Sign 'O' The Times
(1987)*

Hollywood financing and produce the film themselves. As Fargnoli put it, "why go through the process of trying to educate a producer about what Prince was supposed to be doing on film and how to protect his integrity and image, when we knew exactly what he wanted to do?" The three Italians were canny enough to see that the early eighties video boom had paved the way for a new kind of pop film and wanted a correspondingly fat slice of the proceeds. "We didn't want to get to be producers by simply packaging a soundtrack album", said Bob Cavallo. "The music business and the film business are closer than at any time in history and are about to crash into each other."

With a swiftness and economy that rivalled the recording of *Dirty Mind*, they shot the picture in seven weeks for a mere $7 million, less than some episodes of *Dallas* or *Dynasty* cost. Beginning in November, filming had to be quick due to the imminence of Minnesota's severe winter – the state boasts the lowest annual temperature in North America. Production manager Mike Frankovich frequently worked his Californian crew 13 hours a day to complete all outdoor scenes before the snow fell, leaving studio takes and the club scenes (at First Avenue) until January 1984. On set, Prince maintained his customary paranoid aloofness – as Biba Kopf later observed in *NME*, "like all great stars, Prince wants-to-be-alone, but he wants the public to witness his solitude, even sympathise with it." "No one talked to Prince except for the directors and make-up people", said Byron Hechter, a stand-in for Prince fired after talking to a local reporter. "I saw a few people go up to him that weren't supposed to, and Chick told them to go away."

Purple Rain is really a video-age backstage musical, a tragi-comic drama structured by song and performance. A singer called the Kid (Prince) plays with his band The Revolution and keeps away as much as possible from the misery of his home life. Rival band The Time scheme to oust him from his regular gig at First Avenue. And a dusky girl called Apollonia arrives from Louisiana – like Prince's mother Mattie – to try to make it as a singer. Disarmingly true to life, you might think, and if you can trust Prince's version of the truth you'd be right. The film even paints a picture of the tensions and resentments within the real Revolution, portraying the Kid as an arrogant primadonna who dismisses everyone else's input. Certainly Prince was trying to do more here than fashion a diverting entertainment, though if anything it serves to blur permanently any clear boundaries between the reality and the myths of his life. Ultimately *Purple Rain* is a powerful and sometimes troubling self-portrait. As future Pet Shop Boy Neil Tennant wrote in *Smash Hits*, "when Apollonia asks him what he dreams about, he only pouts in reply but his answer is clear: himself." With the guidance of William Blinn and Al Magnoli, Prince was adapting the basic autobiographical facts to suit his own purposes. Thus the Kid's father, like John L. Nelson, is an ex-musician, though he beats up his wife in a way we must assume Prince's father did not. Thus, too, Prince's basement sanctuary in Bernadette Anderson's house is re-created rather fancifully in the Kid's bedroom. Finally, the old "uptown" days of rivalry between Champagne and Flyte Tyme are parodied in the pronounced contrast between the Kid, all purple petulance and brooding rebel-without-a-cause torment,

89

"He wants to communicate",
said William Blinn,
"but he doesn't want you to get too close."

and Morris Day, a camp Richard Pryor-ish lounge lizard who all but steals the show.

The film works surprisingly well. If the dialogue often seems stilted and uncertain, the performances are more than creditable. Prince himself is impressive, an assured presence at all times, while the acting lessons from one Don Armendolia seem to have worked for supporting characters like Jerome Benton, Wendy Melvoin and Jill Jones. Even Chick Huntsberry has a role as the club's bouncer. Inevitably the musical set-pieces, shot in the new year at First Avenue and the Union Bar in Old St Anthony, make the film what it is, but what set-pieces they are. From the opening exhortations of 'Let's Go Crazy' to the climactic self-adoration of 'Baby I'm A Star', *Purple Rain* is the most electrifying promo vehicle ever conceived. "Your music makes sense to no one but yourself", taunts the club's manager Billy, but of course the new-wave hipsters who crowd it out every night prove him wrong, gyrating furiously to 'Computer Blue', swaying dreamily to 'The Beautiful Ones'. Like a crazy salad of Little Richard, James Brown, Jimi Hendrix and Sly Stone, Prince seizes the stage and makes it a parade ground of excessive emotions – the agonised jealousy of 'The Beautiful Ones', the imploring devotion of 'I Would Die 4 U', the wildly frustrated lust of 'Darling Nikki'. (Quite apart from the overt sexism of the film, incidentally, several things in *Purple Rain* betray Prince's uneasy conception of sexuality: most disturbingly, when the Kid first brings Apollonia back to his basement he plays her a tape that sounds like a girl's moans of sexual pleasure. In fact it's a tape of a girl crying played backwards. "It sorta makes me sad", he sighs. For Prince, pain and pleasure remain inextricably bound at all times.)

Of the nine songs which make up the *Purple Rain* album, Prince had written and recorded 'When Doves Cry' and 'The Beautiful Ones' by himself at LA's Sunset Sound. On most of the others, however, The Revolution were for the first time fully involved. Indeed, as dramatised wryly in the film, Prince even used some music that Lisa and Wendy Melvoin (Dez Dickerson's replacement in the band) had written. Not only did the pair substantially compose 'Purple Rain' itself, but they're also co-credited on 'Computer Blue'. Moreover, the band as a whole is credited for the excellent '17 Days', the non-album flipside of 'When Doves Cry'. Clearly Prince had begun to trust someone besides himself. As for the recording sessions, 'Let's Go Crazy' and 'Computer Blue' were cut by the band at Revolution HQ the Warehouse, while 'Purple Rain', 'Baby I'm A Star' and 'I Would Die 4 U' were actually recorded live at First Avenue using Bobby Z's engineer brother David Rivkin. The sessions became even more of a family affair when Lisa Coleman's brother David flew into Minneapolis to add some strings to 'Take Me With U', 'Purple Rain' and 'Baby I'm A Star'. "Years ago, Prince had the idea of the Happy Family", said Wendy Melvoin later. "He'd been alone for years, making all his records by himself. Then he began to talk of having a group of people around him who would all enjoy each other."

The album opens with the same theatrical sense of ceremony as *1999*, parodying in its invocation the kind of preachers the boy king must have heard in his local Seventh Day Adventist Church: "Dearly beloved, we are

Prince at the première
of Purple Rain

ment of those who insist that Prince is first and foremost a brokenhearted balladeer. "Paint a perfect picture/Bring to life a vision in one's mind", he pouts in the song's spoken interjection; "the beautiful ones always smash the picture/Always, everytime . . ." Once again reality fails to match up to the artist's fantasy. The mood changes abruptly with 'Computer Blue', perhaps the least known song from *Purple Rain*. Opening with an implicitly erotic exchange between Lisa and Wendy ("Is the water warm enough?"; "Yes Lisa"; "Shall we begin?"; "Yes Lisa"), it moves through four minutes of rather uninspired thump 'n' grind broken up by a nice semi-classical instrumental section. The closing 'Darling Nikki', however, is like a lost postscript to *Dirty Mind*, a thoroughly lewd and quite droll piece of heavy metal funk which Prince recorded by himself "at a place very close 2 where you live" . . . whatever that means. Its opening scenario of an insatiably horny girl masturbating with a magazine in a hotel lobby must be familiar to many. Less familiar perhaps is the way Prince characteristically changes horses in midstream with the track's closing message. Recorded backwards, it says: "Hello, how are you? I'm fine, because I know that the Lord is coming soon, coming soon . . ." (The writer who called him "a schizoid little tart with a Bible in one hand and his cock in the other" wasn't far off the mark.)

Side Two opens with the song which perhaps more than any other epitomises Prince's experimental genius – 'When Doves Cry'. Nothing else quite like it exists in the history of pop; certainly no more radical piece of music has ever sat at the top of the American charts for so long – six weeks, to be precise. It's a song which somehow

gathered here today/2 get through this thing called life . . ." The song is a jubilant rock 'n' roll redemption of everyday pain and fear, a cry to keep the spirits up when everything looks black. Don't call up that shrink in Beverly Hills, it counsels – "pills and thrills and daffodils will kill" – just GO CRAZY. Like 'Controversy' and '1999', too, it's informed by the implication that the truth, the real joy, lies beyond death – and perhaps beyond madness. Ending up in a Todd Rundgren-style maelstrom of shrieking guitars and synthesizers, the song tumbles into 'Take Me With U', a lightweight duet with Apollonia used on the soundtrack when the couple are taking a hippie-ish ride through the country on Prince's motorbike. More compelling is 'The Beautiful Ones', an immaculate slice of futuristic Smokey Robinson balladry which lends much weight to the argu-

The inner court of Prince's revolution, American Music Awards 1985: Left to right, Lisa Coleman, Brown Mark, Prince, Bobby Z, Wendy Melvoin

manages to combine a charged eroticism with an almost unbearable sadness, a song too which always sounds as if it's about to take off properly but which instead keeps the listener in a unique state of suspense. The main reason for this is that it features no bassline; instead the song is carried simply by its relentlessly spacey electronic drums and sparse keyboard parts. The lyric is superb, intensely concrete yet strangely surreal: "Dream if U can a courtyard/An ocean of violets in bloom/Animals strike curious poses/They feel the heat, the heat between me and U . . ." Despair and yearning fuse in this centrepiece of the film's soundtrack, encapsulating the pain of the Kid's life as he struggles to overcome the frustration and violence he's learned from his parents.

'I Would Die 4 U' is less complicated – a gloriously pounding declaration of love and fidelity – but its lyric still manages to exceed the standard articulation of pop desire. "I'm not a woman/I'm not a man", it opens, "I am something that you'll never understand . . . No need to worry, no need to cry/I'm your messiah and you're the reason why." Once again Prince is toying narcissistically with his own myth: "I'm not a human/I am a dove/I am your conscious/I am love . . ." At least 'Baby I'm A Star', which follows in rapid succession, confines its megalomania to the sphere of pop fame – did anyone ever write such a flagrantly egotistical song and get away with it? A fabulously sassy stomper that defies one to sit still and coerces one into unconditional agreement.

The album closes, of course, with the nine minutes of 'Purple Rain', a draggingly elegaic, Lennonesque rock ballad I've never particularly cared for. Perhaps out of all the LP's tracks it was this classic arena arm-waver of a song which

so endeared *Purple Rain* to the white teen masses of America and helped to shift a stupendous nine million units of it. The record even managed to keep Bruce Springsteen's *Born In The USA* off the Number 1 spot for several weeks, while 'Doves' was the fastest-selling single in Warner Brothers' history. "In some ways *Purple Rain* scared me", Prince subsequently confessed. "It was too successful, and no matter what I do I'll never top it. It's my albatross and it'll be hanging around my neck as long as I'm making music." Released a month before the film, the album sold over a million copies in its first week and helped to convince Warner Brothers' film distributors that the movie might after all be a surprise success. As Steve Fargnoli put it, "the studios had to be educated as to who Prince was, what he meant and whether he had the potential to be an actor on a screen. They had already discovered that if you make a film with David Bowie or Mick Jagger it doesn't necessarily mean you have a big movie." The management were more than confident that they could hype *Purple Rain* into a box-office sensation. "There's something about Prince that piques people's interest a little more than some other artists", said Bob Cavallo shortly before the film's première. "People don't know a lot about him: he's a little *mysterioso* and has a controversial image."

With the album already a huge commercial and critical success, sneak previews of the film garnered the highest approval ratings in Warners' history. Black and white audiences alike gave thumbs-up responses in both San Diego and Denver, setting the Warners bigwigs minds at rest. They want to draw a middle-of-the-road white audience", said William Blinn, and Warners senior vice-president Mark Canton stated that he believed the film had crossover potential. In the event, *Purple Rain* grossed an incredible $60 million in just over two months, taking $20 million more before the box-office started to tail off. Reviews were almost unanimously favourable, though a handful were carefully guarded in their praise. *Newsweek*'s David Denby, for instance, wrote that "Prince is either shrewd enough or exploitative enough (I can't tell which) to gather up the fragments of our culture and send them whirling back at an audience hungry for self-confirmation." (Cavallo, Ruffalo & Fargnoli claimed that "it's a film which comes *from* youth, not one directed *at* them", and there's an element of truth in that.) In some cities the movie outdrew even *Gremlins* and *Ghostbusters*, two of the biggest hits of 1984. Essentially, the marketing was perfect: the album sold the film, which in turn sold the album, which in turn sold the film . . .

In November, a tour began that was to last till April and take in 100 dates from Detroit to Miami. Mobilising a vast troupe of technicians and roadies, it was a rambling affair, shows generally being announced a mere four weeks in advance. By the last performance, in Miami's Orange Bowl on 7 April, 1.7 million people had seen the show and Prince was $20 million richer. In Detroit's Joe Louis Arena, 140,000 people saw it over seven nights, while another 131,000 caught it in Washington DC. As if all that wasn't exhausting enough, the tour was regularly punctuated by unpublicised free concerts for handicapped children. In Washington, a surprise gig at the Gallaudet College for the Deaf saw students being bussed in from all over the state not knowing what they were going to see. Sign language interpreters flashed Prince's lyrics to the crowd. Other performances were given at the Santa Monica Civic in California, at Houston's Texas Southern University, and at Lehman College's Performance Art Center in the Bronx. The tour also served to raise $500,000 for Marva Collins' experimental Teacher Training Institute in Chicago, primarily through the selling of special $50 tickets for "Purple Circle" seats.

It was a formidable show, two hours of dazzling, dizzying tricks that many non-Americans got the chance to see when it was broadcast live to 26 countries just a week before the tour ended. Transmitted via satellite from the Carrier Dome in Syracuse, New York, the set opened fairly predictably with 'Let's Go Crazy', Prince looking outrageously camp with a teased bouffant and a white fur stole over his right shoulder. (Little Richard's kid sister, Julie Burchill called him – Prince had even been offered the lead role in a Little Richard biopic.) Mounted as an ensemble in two tiers – keyboard players and drummer raised behind the three guitarists – The Revolution looked stunning. The costumes seen in *Purple Rain*, designed by a graduate of Paris' Ecole des Beaux Arts called Marie France, had spelt the final end of Prince's jumble-sale legwarmer chic, and the tour wardrobe was more extravagant still – a motley whirl of jewellery and lace, dandy psychedelia and Regency ruffles, suggesting the inner sanctum of a decidedly decadent court: Louis XIV meets Sgt Pepper's Lonely Hearts Club Band, perhaps. "Prince Soir", the teen clones who thronged to the shows called it, while American designer Terri Hyland argued that "Prince

93

represents a great contradiction – a real raw, sexual animal/man with soft, sweet fabric draped around this gyrating body". (Hyland uncannily echoes Lillian Roxon's description of Jimi Hendrix in her 1969 *Encyclopaedia Of Rock*: "This was the Wild Man Of Borneo all right, but crossed with the languid, silken, jewelled elegance of a Carnaby Street fop. It was a very erotic combination, and no doubt a shrewdly calculated one. First layer: noble savage. Second layer: SF acid freak. Third layer: Swinging London dandy. How *could* he lose?") Wendy, too, looked perfect as his new foil – a handsome she-man gallant firing out funk riffs from a blue Rickenbacker. Prince later said of her that "she makes me seem all right in the eyes of people watching . . . when I sneer she smiles".

The set divided loosely into three sections: an opening selection of revamped numbers from *1999*, a long segment of bravura funk and soul, and the bulk of *Purple Rain* following more or less the running order of the LP. The soul portion of the show was easily the most scintillating: the dreamy seduction of 'Do Me Baby' feeding into the insatiable funk of 'Irresistible Bitch' and 'Possessed' – dedicated to James Brown – then resuming on the sublime 'How Come U Don't Call Me Anymore?' (originally a 7" flipside of '1999' and covered divinely by Stephanie Mills). Dressed in a glittering black matador outfit, Prince revealed himself as the exemplary R & B showman that he is, providing a mouthwatering foretaste of the soul revue routines to come in the *Parade* shows the following year. "Does your new man have an ass like mine?", he teased before rolling around the floor in a fit of tortured squeals and whimpers.

On the out 'n' out rock 'n' roll of 'Let's Pre-

tend We're Married', Prince stood hammering the piano looking more like Little Richard than ever, while tour manager Alan Leeds' brother Eric honked along on baritone sax. Then the mood promptly changed again as Prince began a bizarre eight-minute dialogue with God – designed, it seemed, to atone for the heavy sexual content of the show. "I believe in you, I trust you, I'll be good", he pleaded, looking up at a billowing sheet that presumably represented his creator, then turned to his audience and asked: "Do you wanna spend the night?" Ten minutes later, after taking a dry ice bath onstage and romping lustily through 'Darling Nikki', he whined "I'm so confused", only to have "God" reply patiently: "Don't be confused, there's only one Lord . . ." Make of it what you will: Prince's restless quest for guilt-free sex certainly doesn't stop here.

After 'I Would Die 4 U', featuring Prince mincing around in white lace, the show reached its first climax with a ten-minute *tour de force* jam on 'Baby I'm A Star'. Everyone from Apollonia 6 to Jerome Benton to Prince's new protégée Sheila E clambered onstage for this funk showdown, and again the spoof James Brown routines of 1986 were semi-premièred. Even those lovable "dancing security" goons Greg Brooks and Wally Safford were given a few minutes to strut their stuff. Unsurprisingly, the encore was 'Purple Rain', or rather an 18-minute rendition of the song which fell squarely into the rock epic tradition of Led Zeppelin's 'Stairway To Heaven' and Lynyrd Skynyrd's 'Free Bird' and gave Prince ample scope to flex his guitar muscles as he took off everyone from Neil Young to his old idol Carlos Santana.

Prince was at the pinnacle of his fame when the tour ended a week later. With immaculate

Prince onstage with Wendy.

"I was his smile when he didn't want to be",

she said.

"I was a balance for him."

timing he'd stolen up on the heels of a Michael Jackson humiliated by 1984's disastrous *Victory* tour and more or less taken over his audience. "He was just what pop music had been waiting for", I noted in a May issue of the *New Statesman*, "a prancing punk, neither black nor white, whose music didn't simply cross over from a black to a white audience but was in its very inception as much theatrical rock pomp as it was slick soul cool." Others were more suspicious of this chameleonic quality. "Prince covers all bases and annexes none", Ian Penman argued in an *NME* review of the film. "Look through his band – a Devo here, a Joan Jett there, the Adam Ant–Jagger frills and flouncing. Leaf through the songbook – never quite rock 'n' roll, never tee-totally Souled; electronics without the secular alienation of Hip Hop and Rap; big 'P' politics – a mash of grandiose balladry and apocalyptic tone – without the need of recourse to any particular addressee. He's the perfect Everyman for the MTV/New Wave American market . . ." In a sense this is what I'd felt watching the *1999* shows, but things had

A rococo hippie:
Prince as Janis Joplin,
New York 1984
Prince as superbad Sly

changed and Prince very definitely *was* annexing some bases. Strutting soul man, sobbing balladeer, flouncing glam-rocker: how many of these were masks finally seemed irrelevant. "I don't think my music is easily traced back to Motown or Stax-Volt or any other dominant sixties form", Prince had said in 1981, but his grasp of R&B tradition was now sure enough for him to play a few games with those forms. As a "rock" star, simultaneously, he was taking the achievements of Little Richard and Hendrix into another dimension. In Mat Snow's words, "thirteen years after Jeff Beck snarled into Stevie Wonder's *Talking Book* and three years after Eddie Van Halen spattered Michael Jackson's 'Beat It' . . . Prince's far more harmonious hybrids enthral by their taboo-breaking as much as they jar a few diehards." Even Alexander O'Neal, bearer presumably of more than a few grudges against Prince, conceded that "he's brought a boldness out of black entertainers again. Jimi Hendrix and Little Richard *always* dressed bizarre, and now Prince is doing it in a new era".

The new-found mega-fame inevitably brought mixed blessings. "We were pretty much cloistered from it", says Wendy. "We never really realised how big we were until we left, because we never saw it that way: the autographs and the parties and the clubbing, washing in your fame." For Prince, of course, the pressure was greater, and media perception of him began subtly to change as the tour wore on. "Just as, the year before, Michael Jackson had fallen from boy genius to androgynous eccentric", John Rockwell noted in the *New York Times*, "so between 1984 and 1985 public perception of Prince swung from sly charmer to surly misogynist." "The way I am now, I was always", Prince had once said; "I suppose if I lived in California and rode around in limos all

96

LFI

RETNA

the time and had people waiting on me hand and foot, then maybe that could make you change. People with the strongest minds change to some degree." Change or no change, the media diligently fulfilled its "Build 'em up, knock 'em down" role and seized on every possible pretext for making out that he'd become an insufferable megalomaniac. The image of him being escorted to various awards ceremonies by the giant Chick Huntsberry is one that sticks above all from this period. At the American Music Awards in January, we learned, Chick had forbidden anyone to talk to Prince or even look at him; presenters, moreover, were told to back away from him every time he went up to accept a trophy. To cap it off, while all the other stars floated off in a cloud of sanctimonious zeal to record 'We Are The World', Prince went to dance at a Hollywood nightclub called Carlos 'n' Charlie's. Here two of his heavies were arrested after assaulting some photographers. Not exactly a PR triumph, you'll agree.

"Prince can only sing what he feels", piped up Wendy in his defence. "That's why I couldn't imagine him being on the USA For Africa record. I couldn't imagine him singing someone else's lyrics." The fact that Prince had already donated a song called '4 The Tears In Your Eyes' to the USA For Africa LP was no excuse in the hypocritical eyes of the press. He wasn't playing the post-Geldof Pop Star game, and that simply wasn't on. And so began a concerted campaign of tabloid vitriol designed to dislodge Prince from his high and mighty perch: suddenly he was a "little squirt", a "megalomaniac midget", the "potty purple pop star". We learned that behind his back in Minneapolis he was known as "Napoleon" and "the Ayatollah". No doubt he was quite used to being called names, but that can't have made things much easier. Old "friends" joined in with vicious glee. "I liked

him better before", remarked Owen Husney's wife Britt, while Chris Moon opined to one reporter that "he's gotta be one very lonely guy — he's left a trail of broken hearts and broken egos behind him". True, Prince's various body-guards were becoming an increasingly intimidating symbol of power, but he does seem to have been genuinely afraid of a John Lennon-style death. (In any case, Chick Huntsberry was himself subsequently fired for calling Prince a "little prick" to his face! "He's the weirdest guy I ever met", the former wrestler and evangelist told *National Enquirer*. "He feels he's a second Mozart.") William Blinn probably put it most fairly: "It's hard to have that much power and have close friends. It's tough but I don't feel his solitude is harmful to him. He might be alone, but he knows what to do."

"I wanna see my life change", Prince had said when the *Purple Rain* album was released, "and I wanna be there when it changes. I don't wanna just be doing what's expected of me." Much had already changed by the spring of 1985, and many more little revolutions were just around the corner. On top of everything that was happening in his own career, his little empire of protégés and starlets was continuing to expand. After the *Purple Rain* phenomenon, someone wittily dubbed Prince's Midwest hit factory "Miniwood" and projected that it would soon be competing with Honeywell and 3M as Minneapolis' biggest exports. "They come to me with an idea and I try to bring it forth", said Prince of his artists. "I don't give them anything. I don't say, OK, you're gonna do this. I mean, it was Morris Day's idea to be as sick as he was. That was his personality."

Of his original groups, The Time stayed together to cut one last album, *Ice Cream Castle*, in the summer of 1984. Its two semi-decent tracks, 'The Bird' and 'Jungle Love', were fea-

The Glamorous Life,
1984

tured in *Purple Rain*, while the amusingly-titled 'If The Kid Can't Make You Come' may have been intended as a wry comment on Prince. Much of the fire had gone out of the band with the departure of Jimmy Jam, Terry Lewis and Monte Moir, replaced by bassist Jerry Hubbard and white keyboard players Paul Peterson and Mark Cardenas. If the album went gold, reaching Number 24 on the pop chart, any real enthusiasm had dried up and the band fell apart before the *Purple Rain* tour even began. As for Vanity 6, the lady herself had left the Prince camp upon ascertaining the derisory sum she was to be paid – as a professional actress, mark you, and veteran of softcore pornflick *Tanya's Island* – for *Purple Rain*. Thus ended one of pop's great love affairs. "I always felt we'd be like Burton and Taylor", sighed Vanity to one paper. "I can honestly say I love the kid." (To a rather smuttier rag she later disclosed that "as a lover, Prince is the best – I've spoken to many women who've been to bed with him and they all say the same . . .")

Vanity's replacement, Apollonia – née Patti Kotero from Santa Monica – was an ex-girlfriend of David Lee Roth's who'd appeared in a TV mini-series called *Mystic Warrior*. Having got the *Purple Rain* part after some intensive auditions, she sang on the *Apollonia 6* album released in October 1984 but never really became part of a group. "Vanity brought a much stronger, more blatant sexual influence to stuff like 'Nasty Girl'," said Brenda Bennett. "Apollonia has brought a more glamorous appeal – more sensuous and erotic, less slap-you-in-the-face-with-it." The trio only ever made one public appearance, at Prince's tour-opening Detroit concerts in November, and the album – boasting sub-'Nasty Girl' items like 'Sex Shooter' – was pretty tacky. (Of vague interest perhaps is the fact that the LP's UK release

featured a version of 'Manic Monday', subsequently "written exclusively" for The Bangles!) Later the lissome Latin beauty managed to secure a part in the soap opera *Falcon Crest*.

A considerably more talented young woman was one Sheila Escovedo, percussionist daughter of ex-Santana member Pete Escovedo. Sheila had grown up around San Francisco playing in various Bay Area Latin rock groups and even touring for a period with Pete's 24-piece band Azteca. After a 1977 album with him, *Solo Two*, she'd worked as a percussionist with everyone from Jeffrey Osborne and George Duke to Marvin Gaye and Lionel Richie. Introduced to Prince by none other than Carlos Santana, she swiftly became Sheila E and started work on *The Glamorous Life*, a "Starr Company"-produced album released in June 1984. If the sound was basically Prince's, songs like the great title track and 'The Belle Of St Mark' – both singles, and hit ones at that – were leagues above the saucy candyfloss of Vanity/Apollonia 6. A flying visit to play Channel 4's *The Tube* in England put both 'The Belle' and *The Glamorous Life* in the UK charts, and when Prince came to line up support for the *Purple Rain* tour, Sheila was the obvious contender.

"Everything Prince did from the beginning was a plan", says Jimmy Jam. "We just watched it all happen like he said it would. It was really cool." Those long nights of strategy and campaign back in 1977 had finally paid off: Prince was undeniably one of a tiny handful of major superstars, on a par with Jackson and Springsteen. Anyone, though, who figured Prince would now sit back, play it safe, and consolidate that freakish success was completely overlooking his "imp of the perverse".

Chapter Six

Rain Parade

The first thing Prince did after finally coming off the road in April 1985 was release another album. With the pop market already flooded by all manner of artefacts purple it looked like commercial suicide, but that didn't appear to bother him. Moreover, issued without so much as a half-page ad in *Billboard*, *Around The World In A Day* generated a huge buzz by its very absence of promotion.

The album had grown out of the long rehearsal sessions for the *Purple Rain* tour, extending the "family affair" ambience of the earlier album by involving the Revolution to an even greater degree. "It was a group project", says Wendy. "When we'd finished rehearsing at the end of the day, we'd turn on the tape machines and go to work on *Around The World*. The Warehouse nearly turned into our home. While the guys were out playing basketball, Lisa and I would be inside laying down guitar parts, strings, or vocals . . ." The entire LP was recorded in a matter of weeks, most of it at the new Paisley Park studio which had been built in The Warehouse. "I had a sort of FU attitude

making it", Prince told DJ The Electrifying Mojo in a rare radio interview, "meaning that I was making something for myself and my fans, for the people who've supported me through the years. It was like my little letter, and those people are the ones who wrote me back and told me they felt what I was feeling. Record sales and things like that, it really doesn't matter, you know, it keeps the roof over your head and it keeps money and all in these folk's pockets that I got hangin' around here, y'know, but it basically stems from the music . . . I wouldn't mind if I just went broke, y'know, as long as I could play this type of thing."

Many people saw (and still see) *Around The World In A Day* as Prince's "hippie" album, a logical development of some of *Purple Rain*'s sentiments but essentially a neo-psychedelic folly: after the rain comes a Paisley rainbow of bubblegum peace 'n' love. But if to some extent it draws on everything from The Beatles' *Sergeant Pepper* and Jimi Hendrix's *Axis: Bold As Love* to Sly And The Family Stone's *There's A Riot Goin' On* and The Temptations'

'Psychedelic Shack', the album is hardly the flower-power festival most critics initially took it to be. 'America' and 'Tamborine' are pure cold-blooded funk; 'Condition Of The Heart' is an epic sob of a soul ballad; and 'Pop Life' is a beautifully flip critique of the eighties pop climate. But neo-psychedelic is certainly one way of describing songs like 'Raspberry Beret', 'Paisley Park' itself, and the opening (title) track. None of them is terribly good, their charm deriving mainly from their implicit references to such sixties landmarks of pop psychedelia as The Beatles' 'Strawberry Fields Forever' and 'Magical Mystery Tour' and The Small Faces' 'Itchycoo Park'. The influence of The Beatles in particular permeates the LP, though of course Prince made it without the aid of hallucinogenics. ("There is absolutely no person in this band involved with drugs", Wendy told *Rolling Stone*. "We're real militant about that.") The LP was even, like *Sgt Pepper*, intended to produce no singles, although Warner Brothers in the end managed to pressure Prince to release 'Raspberry Beret', 'Pop Life' and 'America'.

The feel of 'Around The World In A Day' itself immediately conjures the spirit of 1967. Lisa Coleman's brother David plays cello and various Eastern instruments – the oud, the dar-buka and some fingercymbals – as Prince invites us on "a wonderful trip through our time/And laughter is all U pay". 'Paisley Park' is like Paul McCartney at his corniest (there's even an undisguised reference to 'Eleanor Rigby') but summarises fairly simply the beatific spiritual vision Prince seems to have had. "Admission is easy, just say U/Believe and come to this/Place

in your heart/Paisley Park is in your heart." 'Raspberry Beret' is catchy bubblegum à la The Beatles' 'Yellow Submarine' or The Lemon Pipers' 'Green Tamborine', a typical Prince story of seduction by some carefree young maiden, with strings arranged by Wendy and Lisa. "On a song like 'Raspberry Beret'," recalls Wendy, "Prince would say 'This needs strings – whatever you think of to make it wonderful, do it.' Susan Rogers, our tech and buddy, would have the tape on the steps of his place when we'd finished, and he'd listen to it in his car. The day he listened to what we'd done with 'Raspberry Beret' and 'Paisley Park' he walked into the studio stone-faced as if he didn't like it. He was doing his best to tease us . . ."

Of all the LP's songs, the most explicit *transcendental* is 'The Ladder', the story of a restless and dissatisfied king who is searching for "salvation of the soul". Ruling the land of Sina-plenty, and loved by a woman called Elektra, he knows he must find "the ladder" – the answers to "how the story started and how it will end". Co-written with his father John L Nelson, the song is like a gospel version of 'Purple Rain', featuring the backing choir of Wendy and Lisa together with Wendy's sister Susannah (briefly Prince's girlfriend) and a certain Taj (probably future Paisley Park signing Taja Sevelle). Shortly after the *Purple Rain* tour ended, Steve Fargnoli had announced to the press that Prince was retiring permanently from live performances: "I asked Prince what he planned to do", he said, "and he told me 'I'm going to look for the ladder'. So I asked him what he meant. All he said was 'Sometimes it snows in April'." Apparently the song's title referred to something

Wendy and Lisa,
who left Prince to record
their own album in
1987

his father had said, but there's even a sketch of a ladder leading to some higher spiritual plane on the cover of *1999*, so clearly it was already a potent symbol for Prince. In a sense the track simply recaps on previously stated spiritual convictions. "I've been accused of a lot of things contrary to this", he's since remarked, "and I just want people to know that I'm very sincere in my beliefs. I pray every night and I don't ask for much. I just say 'thank you' all the time." Second-generation hippie Wendy linked this deep religious sense to the "psychedelia" of the album: "In the psychedelic sixties, people were trying to find an answer through drugs and felt that God was someone who told you 'Don't do this, don't do that.' In this age, we don't feel that. Instead of psychedelia, we explore experience and open up our minds by going into God and into ourselves. You can't become clearer by clouding your mind with drugs."

The more Old Testament-style creator of 'Don't do this, don't do that' meanwhile makes an appearance on the extraordinary closing track 'Temptation'. This is Prince exorcising some fundamentalist guilt, a striptease romp which lustily whoops it up until God Himself performs a quick cameo turn to teach the boy that love is more important than sex. "O silly man, that's not how it works", He announces, "you have to want it for the right reasons." "I do", protests Prince. "You don't", counters his maker. "Now die." Finally, after some bizarre shrieks of pain and remorse, the purple one claims he understands.

"Once you've listened in this deep to this whimsical frolic of a record", wrote Greg Tate in a *Spin* review of *Around The World*, "you

Prince the gigolo, in Under The Cherry Moon

begin to wonder if what we have here isn't a form of self-parody, like say Prince was out to defuse all his stud swagger and charisma in favour of an image more fey." If that analysis holds good for much of the album, it doesn't quite cover the LP's best songs, 'America', 'Pop Life' and 'Condition Of The Heart', none of which have a lot to do with the secret garden psychedelia of 'Paisley Park'. Anticipating the bleak scenarios of 'Sign 'O' The Times', for instance, 'America' is a frantic parody anthem which could have come straight off Sly And The Family Stones's *There's A Riot Goin' On* – "Little sister making minimum wage/Living in a one-room monkey cage/. . . America, America/God shed his grace on thee" – while 'Pop Life' is a brilliant meta-pop commentary riding on an effortlessly sassy funk groove and powered by the drums of Sheila E. 'Condition Of The Heart', finally, is one of Prince's great ballads, an elaborately arranged and orchestrated epic that he recorded by himself at Sunset Sound.

Critical reaction to the record was predictable enough. The story even goes that when Prince unveiled it to the Warners executives he sat toying with a flower and watched the blood drain from their faces. "Prince Rogers Nelson's Lonely Hearts Club Band or Beyond The Valley Of The Purple Doll?", asked Richard Williams in *The Face*. "Is 'Paisley Park' his 'Penny Lane' or his 'Electric Ladyland'? Riddle or put-on? These questions I can live without. Who would not rather go out and have a good time with '1999' than stay home to puzzle over 'The Ladder'?" The bemused put-downs were reminiscent of the hammering Stevie Wonder's *Journey Into The Secret Life Of Plants* had taken in the seventies. "*Purple Rain* fans dropped off and didn't understand what he was doing after that", says Jill Jones. Prince remained non-chalant: it meant more that George Clinton, whose 1984 set at First Avenue had inspired the excellent B-side 'Erotic City', liked the album than that "some mamma-jamma wearing glasses and an alligator shirt behind a typewriter" deemed it foolish. Besides, at the end of the day it went platinum and spawned a Top Ten hit in 'Raspberry Beret' (whose amusingly trippy video was directed by Prince himself).

With *Around The World In A Day* left to fend more or less for itself, Prince turned his attention to ideas for another film. One which particularly attracted him concerned the story of a struggling musician on the Côte d'Azur in the South of France, and after a few weeks' rest at home in Minneapolis, he left with Steve Farg-noli for Paris, a hip noble savage following in the dance steps of such exotic imported blacks as Josephine Baker and Grace Jones. Holed up in a hotel room writing songs by day, by night he roamed the city's nightclubs, and here both the plot of the film and the feel of its soundtrack began to take shape. In July, he and Fargnoli headed south to scout locations, eventually scheduling several weeks of filming around Nice and Antibes with an all-European crew headed by Fassbinder veteran Michael Ballhaus. Writ-ten by first-timer Becky Johnston, the film was initially put in the hands of director Mary Lam-bert, who'd made Madonna's 'Material Girl' video. "I prefer to work with someone who knows exactly what he wants", Lambert said before shooting started; unfortunately she hadn't realised just how much Prince did want, and was

quickly demoted to an advisory role when he decided to take complete control of the film.

In *Under The Cherry Moon*, as the film came to be titled, Prince plays the suavely gigolo-esque Christopher Tracy, a piano player on the Côte d'Azur who falls in love with shipping magnate's daughter Kristin Scott-Thomas. "It's kind of *Pygmalion* in reverse", says Lisa Cole-man. "Instead of creating a high-society dame, it's about a guy trying to loosen up one." Drawing on a wide variety of sources – *Just A Gigolo*, *Summer Holiday*, above all the style of 1920s idols like Rudolph Valentino – the film is a lighthearted and ironic pastiche that never really clicks. As Stuart Cosgrove noted in *New Musical Express*, "Prince is literally *too* involved and *too* concerned with his own screen presence to be taken seriously as a director." Steven Berkoff, flown out to Nice to take over the role of the magnate from Terence Stamp, asked "Who tells the truth to a star?" – certainly, one might reply, nobody on the set of *Cherry Moon*. If the camp interplay between the star and sidekick Tricky (Jerome Benton) threw up the occasional moment of mirth, this time Prince had reached too far: demanding that you pro-duce your first album at the age of 20 is one thing, but directing your second film at 27 is another matter altogether.

The film, panned almost universally, bombed. In its first week, showing in more than 200 theatres across America, it earned a mere $3.2 million, quarter of what *Purple Rain* made in its first weekend. Receipts dropped 50 per cent in the second, plummeting in New York from $600,000 to a mere $270,000. "Another movie like this", wrote Vincent Canby in the

New York Times, "and Prince's revolution will be over." Like Madonna with Shanghai Surprise, the purple autocrat had been too eager to capitalise on the runaway success of a first hit movie. Thankfully the soundtrack album Parade fared better – critically and commercially – though once again Prince flouted market logic and released it less than a year after Around The World. "Some previewers have been describing Parade as a funk-infused refinement of last year's neo-psychedelic Around The World In A Day", reported Billboard, "while others are hailing it as a welcome return to the scaled-down soulfulness of the controversial popster's early style-shaping Dirty Mind." In truth it was a bit of both. If the brilliantly spare minimalism of the first single 'Kiss' suggested the aura of Dirty Mind, the other tracks featured orchestral arrangements even more elaborate than those on Around The World. Billboard's Nelson George saw 'Kiss', 'Girls' and 'Anotherloverholenyohead' as a kind of modern R & B trilogy and applauded the re-emergence of Prince's falsetto, but other writers focussed on the extraordinary atonal string and reed arrangements – courtesy mainly of ex-Rufus arranger Clare Fischer – which suggested the influence of Broadway musicals filtered through the quirky psychedelia of the earlier album. Whichever way you looked at it, Parade was an odd bird. The only simple thing about it was its chic monochrome cover.

'Christopher Tracy's Parade' opens Side One as a busy, bustling invocation. As with 'Around The World In A Day', there is the feeling of being welcomed aboard some magical mystery tour, and Fischer's multi-layered score gives the track a touch of Hollywood epic. The Caribbean-flavoured funk of 'New Position' amounts to little more than a tamely token sex ditty, but 'I Wonder U' conjures up the slightly sinister world of The Beatles' "White Album". 'Under The Cherry Moon', like 'Christopher Tracy's Parade' co-written by Prince's father, suggests the weary decadence of the European chanson tradition, a perfect soundtrack for the film's setting: "If nobody kills me or thrills me soon/I'll die in your arms under the cherry moon . . ." Jump half a century and suddenly you're bumping and grinding to 'Girls And Boys', a lusty outbreak of mid-tempo funk twice as long (five and a half minutes) as any of the curious pieces which precede it. Pushed along by Eric Leeds' grunting sax, the song harks back to LaBelle's 'Lady Marmalade' in its use of sexy French pouting. 'Life Can Be So Nice' instantly returns us to Clare Fischer's eccentric arrangements, juxtaposing trilling pipes against Sheila E's frenetic, almost African-style percussion. (As Barry Walters observed in the Village Voice, "much of Parade breaks down to a complex alliance of percussion and vocals, staggered and interwoven with the sort of intricacy one has come to expect of West African pop.") As a tailpiece, the two-minute instrumental 'Venus De Milo' sounds like what it is – some incidental filler from a soundtrack, lovely but hardly definitive Prince.

The second side kicks off with the pounding 'Mountains', a great song by Wendy and Lisa that could almost be Prince's old heroes Earth, Wind & Fire. With its huge brass arrangement and rapturous, wave-like chorus it stands out as one of the album's most accessible tracks. 'Do U Lie?', like 'Under The Cherry Moon', suggests a tuxedo'd jazz band in the palm court of a grand Cannes hotel. Undoubtedly a nod to John Nelson's jazz influence on Prince, the song is an exquisitely crafted pastiche of the twenties sound. Next up, 'Kiss' is so ineffably simple it almost defies description: arranged by David Rivkin, it's minimalist sex-gospel, a camp Curtis Mayfield cooing and squealing over the dryest mix of drums and keyboards you ever heard. (George Michael slavishly imitated every last trick on his equally irresistible 'I Want Your Sex'.) Wendy's wah-wah guitar solo is another masterstroke, more than qualifying her

for the role she plays in the song's video – a bemused, role-reversed spectator watching the narcissistic male strip. "Women, like girls, rule my world/I said they rule my world", the imp sings; "Act your age, not your shoe size/Maybe we can do the twirl/You don't have to watch *Dynasty* to have an attitude/You just leave it all up to me/My love will be your fool . . ." "'Kiss' is one of his blackest records ever", observed Jimmy Jam as the record raced to the top of all three charts – pop, black and dance; "what that does is it changes programmers' ears. They no longer have that 'well, it's too funky for our station' idea." The only bad thing about the next track, 'Anotherloverholenyohead' is its title: the song itself is one of Prince's greatest, an urgent lover's plea sung over a propulsive dance beat and a brilliantly haunting melody. The closing 'Sometimes It Snows In April', finally, is a seven-minute ballad built around piano and acoustic guitar. Others have found it very moving; personally I think it limp and trite. Only its religious implications and its homo-erotic/narcissistic quality – Prince is singing a

RETNA

Prince in peach, on the Sign 'O' The Times *European tour 1987*

valedictory to Christopher Tracy (a Christ figure?), whom of course he plays in the film – make it remotely noteworthy.

If the pop press gave a pretty unanimous thumbs-up to *Parade* – this writer seemed almost alone in his doubts – Prince himself saw little in it to boast about. "*Parade* was a disaster", he announced in an interview on the TV show *American Heartbeat*. "Apart from 'Kiss' there's nothing on it I'm particularly proud of. The temptation is to go right back into the studio and make a killer album, but I think half the problem with *Parade* was that I recorded it too soon after *Around The World In A Day* and I just didn't have enough good material ready. I'm not gonna make that mistake again." An unduly harsh verdict, perhaps, but one to be expected from such a relentless perfectionist. At least the *Parade* tour which kicked off in the early summer – so much for Prince's "retirement" from the stage – showed him having a ball. It was his best show yet, an exuberant *tour de force* of eroticism, parody and pure flamboyance. Abandoning the luxurious wardrobe of the *Purple Rain* year, the players were stripped down to sharp suits and tuxedos, more Apollo Theatre than Fillmore West. The set, too, dispensed with much of *Purple Rain*'s cosmic slop, mounting a full-scale R & B attack on the senses. It looked and sounded fabulous, and it was all you could do not to sit through the show grinning like a Cheshire cat. "He has become more of a dancer and less of a satyr", wrote the *New York Times*' Stephen Holden of the spectacle. "The concert was a high-spirited funk show with stage choreography and acrobatics that connected Prince more directly than ever to

The "megalomaniac midget" at work

the youthful James Brown. He has obviously decided to stop presenting himself as an icon of controversy."

One of the best dates was on his birthday (7 June) at Detroit's Cobo Arena, where helium balloons were attached to every seat. The show was also filmed, providing lasting documentation of its many delights. Particularly amusing was the interplay between the elfin Prince and his three hefty stooges Jerome, Greg and Wally – trust Prince to get away with using an unashamedly overweight dancer. Jerome Benton proved as invaluable a human prop as he had been for Morris Day in The Time, and musically it was a stunning affair: with The Revolution now fully augmented by hornmen Eric Leeds and Matt Blistan and guitarist Mico Weaver, the sound was looser, jazzier. Mico's playing, especially, freed Prince as a singer and hyper-athletic dancer. Trying to keep up with the costume changes was dizzying: one moment the man was in a lemon yellow suit, turning 'Dance Music Sex Romance' into a cross between Busby Berkeley and The Temptations, the next he was in black leather and Ray-Bans belting out Jerry Lee Lewis' 'Whole Lotta Shakin' Goin' On'. "Some insisted he'd just dumped layer upon layer of pop history into an irresistible catch-all and tarted it up in showbiz razzmatazz", wrote *Melody Maker*, but British audiences were transfixed and enraptured when the show came to London's Wembley Arena for three dates in August. "Whether he's in control or not you have to hand it to the boy", observed David Toop in *The Face*. "He knows how to sort through the post-codes of the day and deliver us from levelheadedness." "If you take any of this

seriously", the boy himself drawled at Wembley, "you're a bigger fool than I am."

If Prince was no longer quite the stellar entity he'd been a year before, he was very probably a happier man. The mania and hysteria which had accompanied the success of *Purple Rain* – one of the ten best-selling albums of all time – had alarmed as much as it had gratified him. Things now were a little calmer, allowing him to indulge and enjoy himself in ways that had seemed impossible for some time. And still few people knew much more about him than they could have found out five years earlier. "No one really knows him that well", says Jill Jones, who's gotten closer to him than most. "People think they do but none of us does." In an otherwise unrevealing interview with *Rolling Stone* in September 1985 – Prince and his management had final vetting rights on the piece – he told Neal Karlen that Susannah Melvoin had asked if he wanted her to drop in "to make it seem like you've got friends coming by". (It's less revealing about the man's loneliness than it is about a man who wants the world to think he has no friends. As Stuart Cosgrove noted, "Prince has learnt all he knows from Howard Hughes: you can never be too secret or too strange; at all costs you must be a very public hermit.") In 1979 the boy wonder had confessed to Minneapolis writer Jon Bream that "when I talk to people, it's almost like a routine. They'll tell you what they want you to know – it's really dumb, and you're supposed to accept that and give your response. I don't like to talk too much. I like to act." Whether anything much had changed in the succeeding seven years is debatable: one suspects that behind much of Prince's chronic shyness

109

On the Parade *tour,*
summer 1986

lies a certain arrogance. "I'm really free and open once I get to know a person", he says, "but when I first encounter someone I'm really cautious, I guess." He is most comfortable around women, claiming that he communicates more naturally with them. "Men are really closed and cold together", he told *Musician*. "They don't like to cry . . . and I think that's wrong." Jill Jones confirms that if you're a woman he'll talk your ear off once he trusts you. "He likes to tell stories", she says, "and he can size somebody up in minutes and take them off brilliantly. He's got an excellent memory for details." As for his ongoing caginess with the media, it was continuing to have its desired effect. The *Rolling Stone* piece notwithstanding, Prince's silence made him as fascinating as ever. "I think he thinks anything he says about the music could prejudice people's attitude to it", says William Blinn. "A little bit of it might be a game. He is actually a very playful individual with a great sense of offbeat humour. There's a little of the Richard Pryor in him."

Minneapolis meanwhile had grown into a major pop mecca, one which revolved around three principal camps: the Paisley Park artists, Jesse Johnson and his acolytes, and the Flyte Tyme production company of Jimmy Jam and Terry Lewis. As Owen Husney put it in January 1986, "people think there are forty or fifty acts here but there aren't. There are just different combinations of the same people." Not everyone was so keen to celebrate the Motownesque "happy family" scenario of 'Miniwood'. "I notice that people are trying to play this 'everybody is helping each other' thing", sneered the surly André Cymone. "In fact it's a fabrication."

But then even Husney – still Cymone's manager at this time – was wary of playing it up too much: "There have been a lot of signings out of here, with labels trying to see what's next and jumping on the bandwagon. That's OK, but I'm trying to be very careful that this doesn't become like the other music places have gotten, like Nashville, where you can drive in and record your album for $29.95 . . ." Prince himself was aware that the happy family picture wasn't quite the whole truth, but sounded a more positive note than Cymone. "There are people that have flown the coop, so to speak", he told The Electrifying Mojo, "and gone off to do their own thing. That's great, and I stand behind them and support them in whatever they do. Contrary to rumours, we're all real tight still."

If Paisley Park wasn't quite a hit factory yet, the $10 million Prince spent on it in 1986 certainly helped to create the right environment for one. Now known as The Complex, the building he'd acquired in May 1984 had turned into something out of the final scenes of a James Bond movie. With concrete walls two feet thick, it housed not only two state-of-the-art recording studios (modelled on his beloved Sunset Sound) but everything necessary for a full live tour. "As you drive out of Minneapolis and reach open fields", says James Todd of Cavallo, Ruffalo & Fargnoli's London office, "there gleaming before you is this space-age building. It looks like the Emerald City in *The Wizard Of Oz*!" Besides the Paisley Park artists, acts who've already used The Complex include Kool And The Gang and World Party, an English group signed to Cavallo, Ruffalo & Fargnoli.

The label itself had seen a fair flurry of activity since *Purple Rain*. Sheila E's second album *Romance 1600* went a lot further than *The Glamorous Life* and also took Marie France's rococo costumes to camp extremes that even Prince had balked at. Although Sheila produced the album herself, Prince co-wrote and guested on the 12-minute dance opus 'A Love Bizarre' and later made a cameo appearance in the video for 'Sister Fate'. Two new signings to the label, The Family and Madhouse, certainly bore out Owen Husney's "same people, different combinations" formula for Minneapolis. The significantly-named Family came together after Prince suggested his saxman Eric Leeds join forces with Susannah Melvoin and Jerome, Jellybean and Paul Petersen from The Time. Eric, originally from Pittsburgh, had sent a tape to Sheila E care of his brother Alan – Prince's tour manager, usefully enough. As a line-up the group looked not unlike The Revolution – multi-racial/sexual, draped in Paisley threads – and *The Family* LP sounded similar too. "The record sounds surprisingly like Prince", observed Morris Day. "I say surprisingly because I thought he'd learned from us to make the different productions more autonomous, to give them more identity." Of the album's tracks, only two – 'Nothing Compares 2 U' and 'The Screams Of Passion' – stood out. Predictably enough, Prince wrote the first and produced the second. Madhouse were more interesting, though again Prince's covert involvement seems likely. (If he writes songs as "Joey Coco", can "Austria Chanel" really be anything but a pseudonym?) Revolving once more around Eric Leeds, Madhouse's *8* was a wacky collection of untitled jazz-rock-funk instrumentals. If commercially it wasn't the most accessible thing Prince has ever released, it was definitely a lot better than the eponymous debut album by Mazarati, a seven-piece Minneapolis group discovered by Brown Mark (they supplied backing vocals on 'Kiss'). Mazarati looked, in Dave Hill's words, "like emissaries from some eerie *Purple Rain* fan convention" – and again only the Prince-penned '100 MPH' amounted to anything more than a feeble emulation of their master's voice. As a songwriter, of course, Prince was achieving huge success: quite apart from covers of his songs by the likes of Chaka Khan, he was notching up Top Ten smashes for Sheena Easton (the wildly erotic 'Sugar Walls') and the post-neo-psychedelic Bangles (the jingly-jangly 'Manic Monday'). Pseudonyms continued to abound: for 'Sugar Walls' he was Alexander Nevermind, a gentle dig at Alexander O'Neal, while for 'Manic Monday' he reassumed the guise of Christopher Tracy. One might almost credit him, too, with Minneapolis band Ready For The World's 'Oh Sheila': as brazen a Prince imitation as any you're likely to hear, it made Number 1 in the USA in the autumn of 1985.

"He's a hard taskmaster at times", says Jill Jones of Prince the Svengali, "a perfectionist when it comes to singing but generally a director and good collaborator." Along with Madhouse's second LP *16*, Jill's eponymous 1987 debut album is one of the more recent Paisley Park releases. With three Prince co-productions ('Mia Bocca', 'All Day, All Night' and 'For Love') and the involvement of everyone from David Rivkin to Clare Fischer, it's another family affair. Jill of course goes back to the *1999*

days, when she was a teenager with peroxide blonde hair. Half-black and half-Italian, she'd become a trusted confidante of Prince's and finally earned a shot at a solo recording. "Prince and I have a lot of spiritual talks", she says. "I'm like his kid – he's watched me grow and sometimes he's so wise." In addition to the three co-productions, Prince co-wrote the droll 'G-Spot' (originally slated for *Purple Rain*) and supplied an old ballad from the *Prince* album, 'With You'. "He's great at getting me in the mood", she says of him as a producer. "He'll want an atmosphere for a song, so he'll guide me along by conversation. We did one song called 'Violet Blue' which is very emotional, and his father was in the studio. We talked about old times and reminisced and it helped the ambience. I felt like Sarah Vaughan singing in the Blue Note club in 1955." If the album didn't fare terribly well, and if Jill wasn't quite the singer she thought she was, it remains one of the most engaging non-Prince releases on Paisley Park. "Shifting between sleaze and tenderness", in *Melody Maker*'s words, its eight songs amount almost to a cross-section of Prince's styles over a decade: in 'Mia Bocca' you can hear the springy synth riffs of the first three albums, in 'With You' the doe-eyed balladeer of 1979, while 'For Love' catches up with the strutting funk of 'Girls And Boys'. Altogether less enthralling is another debut on the label, by a girl who first got a break as an extra on *Purple Rain*. *Taja Sevelle* came out in late 1987 sounding like a self-conscious fusion of Madonna and Sade, and this time even the token Prince song, 'Wouldn't You Love To Love Me?', was pretty feeble. Interestingly, the mix engineer on the session was one Tommy

The Bangles (above) and Sheena Easton, for both of whom Prince wrote Top Ten hits

Vicari. More recent Paisley Park signings include Tony LeMans, ex-Missing Person Dale Bozzio and – most surprisingly – the folk-blues singer Bonnie Raitt, perhaps another of Prince's seventies heroines.

The two other principal "camps" in Minneapolis have both grown out of The Time. Since Jimmy Jam and Terry Lewis notched up their first monster hit with The SOS Band's sublime 'Just Be Good To Me' (1983), everyone from soul stars like Cheryl Lynn and Howard Johnson to pop groups like The Human League have passed through the hallowed portals of their small, innocuous-looking studio. The combination of Jam's love of "soft melodic funk" and Lewis' taste for harder dance music was a marriage made in soul heaven, creating classic records for Change, Alexander O'Neal and Janet Jackson, whose *Control* LP went multi-platinum in the USA in 1986. "Normally we end up working with artists who seem to be the underdog", says Jimmy. "Maybe someone who's had a hit and is in a slump, like The Human League or The SOS Band. We kind of like that role." Already one of the world's most successful production teams, they currently seem to spend more time turning stars down than taking them on. Jesse Johnson, meanwhile – who ironically produced two tracks on Janet Jackson shortly after leaving The Time in the summer of 1984 – has turned himself into a rather insipid version of Prince. Based at his Jungle Love studios, he's not only made two very Prince-like albums, *Jesse Johnson's Revue* (1985) and *Shockadelica* (1986), but has groomed protégées like Ta Mara, a Moroccan-born version of Vanity who moved to Minne-

apolis at the age of seven. *Shockadelica* even helped to rehabilitate the coke casualty Sly Stone, who growled along on the single 'Crazay'. (Also featured on the LP was percussionist William Daugherty, an original member of Prince's first group Grant Central.) Like André Cymone, Jesse is managed by Owen Husney.

1987 was a comparatively low-profile year for Prince, a year that saw some of his greatest music on the double *Sign 'O' The Times* album but one too in which an over-ambitious stage show had to curtail a world tour because of poor ticket sales. Starting it without The Revolution, which had disbanded (whether permanently or temporarily isn't clear) after a final performance in Japan, he made his first imprint with the album's brilliantly creepy title track, a record which stuck out on daytime pop radio like an apocalyptic prophecy. There isn't much to it, really – a hypnotic rhythm track, the occasional ominous bass interjection, and Prince's fragile, diffident rap – but the total effect is indescribably haunting. Cataloguing a series of twentieth-century horrors, Prince makes you feel the end is nigh – the signs seem to be that something very evil is afoot. At the end, in a tone of suppressed panic, he sings of settling down and raising a family "before it's too late". The doom merchant of '1999' is in no mood to party. A masterpiece. The rest of the album, originally entitled *Crystal Ball* and recorded once again at Paisley Park and Sunset Sound, is a chaotically patchy affair. ("Ah, but some of those patches!" *Q* magazine rightly declared.) If Sides 3 and 4 are chock-full of magnificent things, Sides 1 and 2 sound in the main like whimsical out-takes and demos. The

high-spirited 'Play In The Sunshine' is forced and hollow after 'Sign 'O' The Times', while 'Starfish And Coffee', co-written with Susannah Melvoin, could be an afterthought to *Around The World In A Day*. (In a sense the album collates many of the nooks and crannies Prince has explored over the past decade: the James Brown groove of 'Housequake', the Philly smooch of 'Adore', the glorious powerpop of 'I Could Never Take The Place Of Your Man' are just three of them.)

The best songs on the first platter are the dreamy 'Ballad Of Dorothy Parker', with its dirty slap bass, scatterbrained drum programme and Joni Mitchell reference, and the maddened, slow-building 'It'. 'Slow Love' is a seducer's soul serenade that doesn't quite hit the mark, 'Forever In My Life' a droning pastiche of Sly Stone's 'Everyday People'. Only with Side Three's opening 'U Got The Look' do the real gems commence. A duet with the post-'Sugar Walls' Sheena Easton and a Top 5 hit in America, it's a writhing, hissing dance monster about the battle of the sexes, that "nasty little world" of teen lust and narcissistic parading captured so well by Vanity 6. "Boy versus girl in the World

Jill Jones, whose Paisley Park album was released in 1987:

"No one really knows Prince that well. People think they do but none of us does."

Series of Love", announces Prince, and in the excellent video for the single he and Sheena stake each other out, strutting about in an elaborate dance of challenge. "I've never seen such a pretty girl/Look so tough, baby/U got that look . . ." In the next song, 'If I Was Your Girlfriend' (also a single), the game has changed completely, and Prince has become a lover so desperate for real intimacy that his voice virtually undergoes a sex change: "If I was your girlfriend would U let me dress U/I mean, help U pick out your clothes before we go out . . ." The matter is complicated further by the fact that the vocal is credited to one "Camille", a mysteriously asexual being invented by Prince as yet another perverse disguise. (Indeed, 'Girlfriend' and two other tracks from *Sign 'O' The Times* were originally scheduled to appear on a Paisley Park album by this Prince "relative". The project was scrapped but not before the LP had been given a Warner Bros catalogue number.) Thus the track, an itchily slow funk grind, becomes a riot of distortion and schizoid metamorphosis: the lead vocal speeded up, backing vocals slowed down, keyboards recorded backwards. "The song's agony", wrote Simon Reynolds in the *New Statesman*, "is that of the spirit chafing against the strait-jacket of sexual energy. Of any identity. In Prince's mad, scatty voice we glimpse the dizzying possibility that the ultimate goal of desire is not to be *human* at all . . ." If the cosily chatty details of the song – hairdos, breakfast, going to the movies – rather argue against Reynolds' interpretation, there's nonetheless a singular sense here of Prince exceeding what Stephen Heath termed "the sexual fix". More than just another feather in Prince's polysexual cap, the voice of "Camille" might just be the real imp struggling to get out.

'Strange Relationship' – also credited to Camille – is another redefinition of sexual relations, if a far less acute one. "Baby I just can't stand 2 see U happy", he sings; "more than that I hate 2 see U sad." A contagiously catchy song Prince had played to *Rolling Stone*'s Neal Karlen back in August 1985, it's about the miseries of jealousy and possession: "The more U love me the more it makes me mad." 'I Could Never Take The Place Of Your Man' could almost be *Dirty Mind*'s 'When You Were Mine' revisited, an effortless classic of 4/4 skinny-tie pop which for some reason turns into a kind of sub-Grateful Dead West Coast jam before resuming its powerpop riff for the fade. The West Coast feel continues with Side Four's opener 'The Cross', to date Prince's most explicitly religious song: "there'll be bread 4 all of us", he cries, "if we can just bear the cross". Opening gently with Prince singing over acoustic guitar – the dust cover's image of him as a bespectacled, Buddhistic devotee comes to mind – the track builds to an intense rock crescendo. Next up, the penultimate 'It's Gonna Be A Beautiful Night' acts as a kind of swansong for The Revolution – a nine-minute funk workout co-written by Matt Fink and Eric Leeds and recorded live at a 1986 gig in Paris. It's nothing special, but with Sheila E on percussion and Jill Jones and Susannah Melvoin sharing lead vocals it's a nice way to say goodbye to the family. 'Adore', finally, is one of Prince's great pure soul outings, six-and-a-half minutes of swooning, multi-tracked vocal group acrobatics that pays tribute to everyone from

The Flamingos to The Temptations to The Delfonics to Blue Magic. Genius.

With the members of The Revolution gone their separate ways – Wendy and Lisa to record a sadly underrated album released here on Virgin – Prince set about rounding up a new troupe of musicians and dancers to take *Sign 'O' The Times* on the road. Retaining Fink and Leeds, together with Greg Brooks and Wally Safford, he brought in Sheila E on drums, Mico Weaver as principal guitarist, keyboard player Boni Boyer and dancer Cat Glover, plus a bassist called simply Seacer. At the same time, a brilliant stage set was designed and built at The Complex, one that featured a 42nd St-style scene of neon sleaze and tenement backdrops – signs of the times, no less. In April, both set and band winged their way over to Birmingham's National Exhibition Centre for an intensive month of rehearsals preparatory to a European tour. The British press had a ball trying to snap pictures of Prince in the Warwickshire mansion he'd rented, but the rehearsals went smoothly and the tour – setting aside the fact that two Wembley Stadium dates were cancelled – was a triumph. Exactly why the London dates were cancelled remains a mystery: while the principal reason given was the appalling summer weather, the rumour that too few tickets had been sold seemed too persistent to be dismissed out of hand. For those British fans once again disappointed, an 85-minute film shot in part at the Rotterdam show recently opened over here to general acclaim. Called simply *Sign 'O' The Times*, its live footage is intercut with studio film shot at The Complex, primarily to give fans a close-up view of Prince and band that they normally wouldn't have, but also to impose a somewhat spurious plot-line on the song sequence. Beginning with Prince singing 'Sign 'O' The Times' alone on a stage filled with dry ice, the show concentrates almost entirely on songs from the album, punctuated by slightly unnecessary vignettes of street life. If it can't quite do justice to the full power the 10-piece band managed to cook up in Europe, at least it shows what a difference the likes of Sheila E and dancer Cat Glover made to the basic Prince experience. Cat especially is a marvellously erotic foil to Prince's own exhibitionism. In America the movie had the desired effect, putting Prince back on the map when the rumours said the show was too expensive to take on tour in America.

More rumours, finally: this time that yet another album was slated for imminent release around January 1988. At the time of writing it hasn't appeared and probably never will, since "The Black Album" (as it's code-named) is a collection of hardcore funk out-takes so wantonly obscene it makes *Dirty Mind* sound like the Jackson 5. Still, the running order is: 'Le Grind', 'Cindy C', 'Dead On It', 'When 2 R In Love', 'Bob George', 'Superfunkycalifragisexi', '2 Nigs United 4 West Compton', and 'Hard Rock In A Funky Place', the last a song which has been knocking around the Prince vaults for some years. As for 1988, nothing is certain other than that Prince has the usual surplus of material available for release. Just a few of the other recorded tracks as yet unused include: 'Joy And Repetition', 'The Place In Heaven', 'Witness', 'Can't Stop', 'Neon Telephone', 'Movie Star', 'We Can Funk', 'Girl Of My Dreams', 'Databank', 'Crystal Ball', 'Funny You Should

*Prince as religious
devotee, 1987*
*The high heel collection
on the* Sign 'O'
The Times *tour 1987*

couldn't talk to me or find out much about me they started making things up", he says. "I'm supposed to be a mysterious person but I'm not mysterious." Yet peculiarly remote from the pop process he is, which is why we're all so mesmerised. Not remote like Michael Jackson, whose music becomes more disembodied and antiseptic the more he withdraws into himself, but like somebody who simply doesn't operate on pop's terms. ("Today people don't write songs" is all he'll say about contemporary pop; "they're a lot of sounds, a lot of repetition . . .") What he's done, apparently instinctively, is defy all boundaries, all fixes. In the fine words of Simon Reynolds, "Prince alarms us because he's either too religious or too frivolous for words. He's floated free of roots or use value into an aristocratic, aerial domain of licence and luxury – an orgy of chaotic stylistic miscegenation . . ."

Of course, many have failed to appreciate Prince's free-floating one-man orgy. As black writer Brenda Connor-Bey wrote in the March 1981 issue of *Uptown*, "When we were growing up, the kind of prince offered to us was realistic in that he would not be charging up to us on a white horse or carrying us off to a castle. Instead, he was a struggling brother, one we'd have to work with but whose values and morals had those princely qualities found in the old fairytales. But what is being offered to our young adults today as the type of prince they should either emulate if a manchild or gravitate towards if a young black woman? A young black rocker from Minnesota who bares his small, underdeveloped chest in front of any audience and sings in a falsetto voice." No Citizen's Council redneck could have put it better.

Call', 'Last Heart', 'There Are Others Here With Us', 'Old Friends 4 Sale', 'Wonderful Ass' and 'Our Destiny'. Two film projects which could be on the cards are a *Purple Rain* sequel called *Dream Factory* and a remake of Czech director Milos Forman's 1965 *Loves Of A Blonde*, to which Prince bought rights in 1987. "Prince is just Prince", Owen Husney once helpfully observed; "an enigma." If we've learned anything about the Minneapolitan imp in ten years it's that the moment we know something about him he's already changed into something else: we can't grab a hold of this protean sprite. He is someone who dances among all forms and references and settles on none of them. Enigmatic perhaps not – "when people

"I'm not a woman,
I'm not a man/I am something that you'll never understand."

Prince is just Prince, then. An imp of pop
perversity who continues to charm, seduce, disturb, intoxicate.
"I work a lot", he says. "I'm trying
to get a lot of things done so I can stop for a while.
Everyone's afraid I'm gonna die!"

PRINCE

A UK DISCOGRAPHY

(By Fred Dellar)

SINGLES

1979 'I Wanna Be Your Lover'/'Just As Long As We're Together' (WEA K17537)★
1980 'Sexy Dancer'/'Bambi' (WEA K17590)★
1981 'Do It All Night'/'Head' (WEA K17768)★
1981 'Gotta Stop (Messin' About)'/'Uptown' (WEA K17819)
1981 'Gotta Stop (Messin' About)'/'I Wanna Be Your Lover' (WEA K17819)
1981 'Controversy'/'When You Were Mine' (WEA K17866)★
1982 'Let's Work'/'Ronnie Talk To Russia' (WEA K17922)★
1983 '1999'/'How Come U Don't Call Me Anymore?' (WEA W9896)★
1983 'Little Red Corvette'/'Lady Cab Driver' (WEA W9688)

1983 'Little Red Corvette'/'Lady Cab Driver'/'Automatic'/'International Lover' (WEA W9688T)
1983 'Little Red Corvette'/'Horny Toad' (WEA W9436)
1983 'Little Red Corvette'/'Horny Toad'/'DMSR' (WEA W9436T)
1983 'Let's Pretend We're Married'/'All The Critics Love U In New York' (WEA W9613)★
1984 'When Doves Cry'/'17 Days' (WEA W9286)
1984 'When Doves Cry'/'17 Days'/'1999' (WEA W9286T)
1984 'When Doves Cry'/'17 Days'/'1999'/'DMSR' (WEA W9286T double-pack)
1984 'When Doves Cry'/'17 Days'/'1999'/'DMSR' (WEA W9286C cassette-single)

1984 'Purple Rain'/'God' (WEA W9174)★
1984 'Purple Rain'/'God' (WEA W9174P picture disc)
1984 'I Would Die 4 U'/'Another Lonely Christmas' (WEA W9121)
1984 'I Would Die 4 U'/'Another Lonely Christmas'/'Free' (WEA W9121T)
1984 '1999'/'Little Red Corvette' (WEA W1999)★
1984 '1999'/'Uptown'/'Controversy'/'DMSR'/'Sexy Dancer' (WEA W1999C cassette-single)
1985 'Let's Go Crazy'/'Take Me With U' (WEA W2000)
1985 'Let's Go Crazy'/'Take Me With U'/'Erotic City' (WEA W2000T)
1985 'Paisley Park'/'She's Always In My Hair' (WEA W9052)

1985 'Paisley Park'/
'She's Always In My Hair'/
'Paisley Park' (WEA W9052T)
1985 'Paisley Park'/
'She's Always In My Hair'
(WEA W9052P picture disc)
1985 'Raspberry Beret'/
'Hello' (WEA W8929)★
1985 'Pop Life'/'Girl'
(WEA W8858)★
1986 'Kiss'/'Love Or Money'
(WEA W8751)★
1986 'Kiss'/'Love Or Money'
(WEA W8751P picture disc)
1986 'Mountains'/'Alexa De
Paris' (WEA W8711)★
1986 'Mountains'/
'Alexa De Paris'
(WEA W8711TW white vinyl 10″)
1987 'Girls And Boys'/
'Under The Cherry Moon'
(WEA W8586)
1987 'Girls And Boys'/
'Under The Cherry Moon'/
'Erotic City' (WEA W8586T)
1987 'Girls And Boys'/
'Under The Cherry Moon'/
'She's Always In My Hair'/
'17 Days' (WEA W8586F double-pack)
1987 'Anotherlover-
holenyohead'/'I Wanna Be
Your Lover' (WEA W8521)★
1987 'Sign 'O' The Times'/
'La La La La He He He He'
(WEA W8399)★

1987 'If I Was Your
Girlfriend'/'Shockadelica'
(WEA W8334)★
1987 'If I Was Your
Girlfriend'/'Shockadelica'
(WEA W8334TP picture disc 12″)
1987 'If I Was Your
Girlfriend'/'Shockadelica'
(WEA W8334C cassette-single)
1987 'If I Was Your
Girlfriend'/'Shockadelica'
(WEA W8334E coloured vinyl)
1987 'U Got The Look'/
'Housequake' (WEA W8289)★
1987 'U Got The Look'/
'Housequake'
(WEA W8289TP picture disc 12″)
1987 'U Got The Look'/
'Housequake'
(WEA W8289C cassette-single)
1987 'I Could Never Take
The Place Of Your Man'/
'Hot Thing' (WEA W8288)★
1987 'I Could Never Take
The Place Of Your Man'/
'Hot Thing'
(WEA W8288TP picture disc 12″)
1987 'I Could Never Take
The Place Of Your
Man'/'Hot Thing' (WEA
W8288C cassette-single)

*(★ indicates that the same titles also
appeared on a 12″ version with the catalogue number bearing an additional 'T')*

1980 *Prince* (WEA K56772)
1980 *Dirty Mind*
(WEA K56862) re-released
1981 *Controversy* (WEA K56950)
1983 *1999*
(WEA 92 3809–1 single album)
1983 *1999*
(WEA 92 3720–1 double album)
1984 *Purple Rain* (WEA 925
110–1) available also in purple vinyl
1985 *Around The World In A
Day* (WEA 925 286–1)
1986 *Parade* (WEA 925 395–1)
1986 *Dirty Mind*
(WEA K39393) budget release
1987 *Sign 'O' The Times*
(WEA WX 88)

In the States, a 1978 album *For You* is
available on WEA BSK 3150, while
some early demos appeared on a 1986
release titled *The Minneapolis Genius*
(HPL 3223), though this album has been
disowned by his royal purpleness.